Teaching Teenagers

Model activity sequences for humanistic language learning

Herbert Puchta and Michael Schratz

Pilgrims

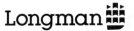

Longman

Longman Group UK Limited,
Longman House, Burnt Mill, Harlow,
Essex CM20 2JE, England
and Associated Companies throughout the world.

Published originally under the title "Handelndes Lernen im Englischunterricht 2 – Praxisbuch", Reihe Forum Sprache, Max Hueber Verlag, Munich, Federal Republic of Germany. Authorized translation by Longman Group UK Limited, England.

© 1984 by Max Hueber Verlag Munich
English translation © Longman Group UK Limited 1993

This book is produced in association with Pilgrims Language Courses Limited of Canterbury, England.

First published 1993
Set in 10/12 Cheltenham Linotronic
Produced by Longman Singapore Publishers (Pte) Ltd
Printed in Singapore

British Library Cataloguing in Publication Data

Puchta, Herbert
  Teaching Teenagers: Model Activity Sequences
  for Humanistic Language Learning
  I. Title   II. Schratz, Michael   III. Lindstromberg, Seth
  428.3

ISBN 0 582 03763 8

Illustrations
Cover illustrated by Mark Dobson

A letter from the Series Editors

Dear Teacher,

This series of teachers' resource books has developed from Pilgrims' involvement in running courses for learners of English and for teachers and teacher trainers.

Our aim is to pass on ideas, techniques and practical activities which we know work in the classroom. Our authors, both Pilgrims teachers and like-minded colleagues in other organisations, present accounts of innovative procedures which will broaden the range of options available to teachers working within communicative and humanistic approaches.

We would be very interested to receive your impressions of the series. If you notice any omissions that we ought to rectify in future editions, or if you think of any interesting variations, please let us know. We will be glad to acknowledge all contributions that we are able to use.

Seth Lindstromberg
Series Editor

Mario Rinvolucri
Series Consultant

Pilgrims Language Courses
Canterbury
Kent
CT1 3HG
England

Herbert Puchta

Michael Schratz

Herbert Puchta has been involved in English Language Teaching since the early 1970s. He has a PhD in Language Teaching Pedagogy and has co-written a number of successful textbooks and resource books including *Conrad and Company* (for younger learners), *Creative Grammar Practice* (in the Pilgrims Longman Resource Books series) and *Pictures in Action*. Herbert is a Master Practitioner of Neuro-Linguistic Programming and has led workshops and seminars in many different countries on the application of psychological and neurological findings to the language classroom. He is currently Professor of English at the Pädagogische Akademie in Graz and is also involved in a research project on the learning styles and strategies of young learners.

Michael Schratz trained as a teacher in lower and upper secondary education and got his doctorate in Education and Psychology. He worked in Bristol (UK), teaching German in secondary schools and adult education classes. In Austria he taught English in various kinds of schools and became involved in teacher training and textbook writing. As a member of a Council of Europe expert group he was involved in evaluation projects in a number of countries. He has conducted qualitative research on communication and personality in language learning and has published several books and articles on foreign language methodology. He is currently Associate Professor of Education at the University of Innsbruck.

Contents

THANKS

We would like to thank:

The students in the trial classes whose enthusiasm, spontaneity and energy we hope will be at least partly evoked for you as you read this book.

The many colleagues in staffrooms and teachers' workshops whose comments and feedback we found so helpful.

Edith Rainer, our typist, who never lost her patience through all our many rewrites.

Uwe Mäder of Langenscheidt-Longman for his encouragement and support.

Robin Davis, who – having read the German version of this book – remarked that it was a pity that it didn't exist in English.

Mario Rinvolucri for his support in general. Also his judgment that our book contained 'lesson plans and historical accounts and juicy little bits of comment that rise like Venus from the waves' which greatly encouraged us to press forward with an improved version in English.

Tessa Woodward for her comments on one chapter and a helpful telephone conversation about it.

Kim Cooley and the late Tracy Terell of the University of California, San Diego, who provided us with an American perspective.

Brigit Viney for her comments and questions.

Seth Lindstromberg for his valuable support and involvement in all the different stages of the manuscript. It is mainly due to Seth that the English version reads so much better than the German original.

Herbert Puchta
Trofaiach, Austria

Michael Schratz
Natters, Austria

April 1992

Preface

In *Teaching Teenagers* Herbert and Michael present nine 'units', each one being a sequence of EFL activities which develop three mutually supporting kinds of skills: linguistic, social and learning. These sequences are ones that you can adapt to work with other texts and topics than the ones featured here. Additionally, each unit tells the story of how a particular sequence of activities unfolded in a real class. Thus, the book is written largely in story form. It also includes verbatim transcripts from key lesson stages, photographs from the trial classes, copies of materials used, teachers' comments on the lessons and samples of student writing (the original wording of which has been copied in clearer handwriting).

In the context of the Pilgrims Longman series this book has the special purpose of demonstrating how individual activities and techniques can be woven together across several successive class meetings in order to work towards long-term goals. Along the way, *Teaching Teenagers* offers up a wealth of teacherly know-how. Just one example of this is using music as a kind of 'bookmark' in a sequence of activities (See Unit 7, pages 88 and 91).

Read and enjoy.

Seth Lindstromberg
Canterbury, 1992

Introduction

BEGINNINGS

This book is the result of a long process whose starting point was our widespread discontent with life at the 'chalkface' in secondary schools.

Along with many colleagues and teacher trainees, we wondered why it was so hard to achieve a good learning atmosphere among teenagers in schools. In particular, why were liveliness, humour and flashes of inspiration much more common in groups of adults than in groups of young people? And why should communicative language teaching work much more smoothly with adults than with teenagers?

On the face of it, there were clear answers. Teenagers are often much less motivated to learn. After all, the goals and ends seem much more distant. Additionally, teenagers typically have a low awareness of the social skills basic to cooperative interaction.

It began to seem to us that there were ways of addressing both these problem areas. Firstly, it seemed probable that – by linking language teaching more closely to students' everyday experience – a teacher could make the end goals of language learning seem nearer and more motivating. Secondly, we realised that while communicative language learning depends on students possessing basic social skills, it also fosters these same skills.

We drew two main conclusions from these thoughts. The way forward lay in making our language teaching more personally relevant, in a word, more 'humanistic'. Additionally, it seemed to us that the effectiveness of communicative language learning in a given class of teenagers ought to grow snowball fashion, provided a teacher is able to surmount initial difficulties in introducing it.

There seemed, though, to be a third obstacle to introducing communicative language learning in secondary schools. This was: how could communicative methods be made compatible with a clearly defined linguistic syllabus?

We wondered if these three obstacles were as real and formidable as they seemed on the surface. We decided to find out. We began by looking closely at the instances where language teaching worked well in teenage classes. Our approach was to try first of all to observe and describe in detail the steps involved in this or that method or technique and then to judge whether it worked or not. We decided to leave the matter of trying to understand *why* something worked or not till afterwards. We are sure, now, that this enabled us to see more during our lesson observations and to come to sounder conclusions afterwards.

Following on from these observations we planned nine activity sequences, lasting several hours each, which would use a humanistic teaching methodology. Although all of the sequences, or units, share a basic set of aims (e.g. making content personally relevant), we designed each one to deal particularly with one or two problems less well-covered in the other units. Thus, for example, Unit 1 describes how we tackled the basic problems of:

- how to introduce humanistic language learning to students familiar only with traditional teaching
- how to make a mundane topic interesting.

After planning these trial units, our next step was to look for teachers willing to try out our ideas and allow us to sit in and record what happened. Doris Friehs, Angela Horak and Andrew Skinner took up the challenge and, thanks to them and their students, the next period of observation was enjoyable as well as fruitful. On the basis of what we learned from these first trials, we taught several of the units ourselves with classes of our own.

The final stage was the analysis and discussion of our mass of observation notes, photographs, audio-recordings (both of classes in session and of inter-views with teachers and students), samples of students' written work and, finally, comments offered by colleagues and trainee teachers to whom we had described the units and shown our observation notes.

The end result is this book, a distillation of what we experienced and what we have learned.

THE SETTING OF THE TRIAL CLASSES

All the teaching took place within the Austrian school system. One unit (Unit 8 *The theatre of the absurd*), was done with an advanced class of seventeen- and eighteen-year-olds. The rest of the units were trialled with lower intermediate thirteen- to fourteen-year-olds. The schools we worked in approximate to the British comprehensive or the American and Canadian high school.

ORGANISATION OF EACH UNIT

Each unit begins with a summary of the unit's aims, the language areas and skills covered, the time it took, the level and size of the trial class, the materials used, the background and rationale and the sequence of activities followed. The main part of each unit is a step-by-step description of what actually happened in the class, along with comment and explanation. Given the huge amount of interesting material we had gathered during the trials, we had to make some very hard decisions about what to include. Our basic aims have been to give a concise, useful and honest account of what really happened in our classes as well as to describe methods and techniques that you can adapt and apply in yours.

PROCESS IN TEACHING AND LEARNING

When teachers talk about teaching among themselves they often focus on the *what* rather than the *how*. They say things like, 'How far have you got in Unit X?' or 'We did up to Exercise Y'. How they used this material is typically unmentioned. Obviously, it is easy to think of teaching in terms of a countable quantity of words, structures and so forth. It is difficult, on the other hand, to characterise it in terms of process. Yet, as little discussed as it is in comparison with language content, the process of teaching and learning is vital. For one thing, the process by which new information is presented or encountered is a fundamental factor in how easily this information can be recalled.

So what is the teaching/learning process and what makes it bad or good? In our view, process in teaching and learning is principally a matter of *the quality of communication* between teacher and students and, especially, between students. If the participants are being both frank and considerate, independent yet cooperative, and are speaking willingly and comprehensibly to particular listeners about things that matter to them both, then the quality of communication is high.

Our attention to detail in describing and presenting instances of authentic classroom communication stems from this view and is designed to clarify how to raise the quality of communication. However, it is not our aim to prescribe rigid procedures for managing the teaching/learning process. What we do hope to offer is a range of well-contextualised insights that can help you focus on the *how* of teaching, whatever your situation.

STATEMENT OF BELIEFS

There is a concept, long-established in the German-language literature on pedagogy, which translates into English as 'social learning', and which underlies our fundamental view about our vocation as language teachers. It consists of the following beliefs:

- The successful and socially well-integrated learner possesses a set of abilities and attitudes which might be called 'cooperative independence in learning'. This is the ability to learn either independently or cooperatively, according to the situation. It is one of the most important results of a successful education.
- A student's progress towards cooperative independence in learning is a long-term goal, requiring continual, patient and thoughtful motivation from teachers.
- To attain cooperative independence, students need to feel able to share their feelings within the context of regular instruction. Such sharing is essential if students are to develop the ability to empathise. This, in turn, is prerequisite to understanding others' behaviour and reacting with tolerance and humanity.
- All participants, teacher and students, should be able to give each

other feedback in a non-judgmental way, so that students are able to openly discuss their own and each other's behaviour and its motives and consequences. Additionally, a steady flow of feedback among and from learners is hugely important to teachers in gauging the appropriacy of content and process of their teaching. This is why student–teacher, teacher–student and student–student feedback plays such a large part in our method.

- Students should be involved in the discussion and negotiation of instruction processes and of group interaction in general. In this book, we call such discussions *meta-discussions* to distinguish them from discussions about language or other topics. Having a voice in the determination of process is an important element in learner independence and, in our experience, greatly fosters constructive attitudes and behaviour.
- Effective foreign language learning can *always* foster language ability and social skills simultaneously.
- Communicative language teaching can work within the context of a clearly defined syllabus. Indeed, most of the time spent on *non*-communicative activities is time and opportunity wasted.
- It is true that teenagers are often less motivated than both younger children and adults. Also, they frequently present outright discipline problems. This is partly due to teachers having missed opportunities to build bridges between what they want to or have to teach and their students' worlds of thought and experience. It is, however, almost never too late to construct these bridges. By doing so you can, by degrees, bring apathetic and unruly students into full and willing participation in classroom learning.

All of these beliefs have been strengthened by our work in connection with making this book.

WHO IS THIS BOOK FOR?

- It principally concerns teaching a foreign language to teenagers, mainly, though not exclusively, in long-term, non-intensive programmes of instruction. However, many of the methods and techniques described here are also of direct relevance to teaching adults in more intensive programmes.
- The provision of broad and definite contexts renders *Teaching Teenagers* an accessible resource for preservice and beginning teachers. It is also useful reading for people on practice-based EFL teacher training courses, or for students working as language assistants.
- Readers undertaking a more theoretical course of training, perhaps at a university or other state-run institution, will find that this book provides a bridge between the world of pedagogical theorising (e.g.

about the merits of humanistic approaches) and how things actually turn out in a particular classroom on a particular day.

- Experienced teachers will find the book helpful, not just for its diverse insights at the level of approach and method but also for its sustained and convincing exposition of how humanistic teaching can be combined with nuts-and-bolts language work.
- Bilingual teachers of monolingual classes or groups will find that the issue of the use of the mother tongue in class gets realistic attention.
- State school teachers everywhere will find this book addresses the most fundamental issues of this situation in a challenging way.

HOW TO USE THIS BOOK

The units in this book can be read in any order. Beginning or pre-service teachers may find it easiest to start with Unit 1 *Young people and pets*, as it is this unit which describes the gradual implementation of the communicative approach in a class that had been taught non-communicatively for their first two years of English. In particular, it is the beginning of a strand of thought running throughout the book, that is, how group cooperation can be encouraged and can motivate the students more and more.

However, in reading the book, remind yourself that we are not asking you to turn your ideas about teaching, much less your personal teaching style, upside-down from one day to the next. We are suggesting a direction in which to *gradually* broaden your approach to teaching.

- Start by trying out activity types and techniques that seem to fit best with your present teaching style.
- Keep careful track of your students' reactions, and your own!
- If you choose to implement only individual elements from a unit, read through the whole of the unit in question first in order to get a clear idea of the original context.
- Before you teach a whole unit, carefully plan any adaptations to suit the level and interests of your class. Run through the procedure mentally as if you were actually in your class watching it being taught or were 'up front' teaching it yourself. Maintain a non-judgmental attitude while doing this. Avoid quick reactions like, 'This will never work in my class!' Instead, make a note of any potentially difficult phases and adapt what you are planning to do accordingly.

We predict that each time you try out and take on board a new technique or succeed with a new type of activity, more of the other activities in the book will seem feasible and appealing, and that trying them out will increase your confidence and ability to plan for long-term social learning as well as short-term linguistic aims.

Young people and pets

Teaching communicatively in a traditional class

LEVEL
Upper elementary – intermediate

TIME
6–8 hours

TRIAL CLASS
Twenty-four thirteen- to fourteen-year-old lower intermediate learners in their third year of English; three fifty-minute lessons a week

AIMS
Laying the groundwork for deeper communicative work and generally raising students' interest in English; improving teacher–student rapport; developing students' capacity for empathy; integrating turned-off students; making a mundane topic interesting

Language areas and skills
Present simple; expression of likes and dislikes; oral fluency; basic language for speculating about people and things; listening; reading; writing

Materials
Stage 1: Poster of pictures of young people, pets and homes, with labels (Fig. 1.1, p. 10)
Stage 2: Hand-out of questions about teacher (Fig. 1.2, p. 13)
Stage 9: Students' photos of pets; OHP transparency or hand-out of a model group report (Fig. 1.7, p. 19)
Stage 12: Hand-out of pictures of animals (Fig. 1.9, p. 21)
Stage 13: Hand-out of useful language (Fig. 1.10, p. 22)
Stage 14: Hand-out about reactions to animals (Fig. 1.11, p. 22)
Stage 15: Posters to stimulate discussions (Figs. 1.12–1.13, pp. 23–4)
Stage 16: Paper, scissors, glue, pens and pictures for making posters (students can bring in pictures). Leftover bits of wallpaper can be used to make posters and collages and can often be obtained free from shops

BACKGROUND AND RATIONALE

Sooner or later every teacher inclined to using communicative methods faces a new class deadened by their experience with poor teaching. In this situation you have to do a great deal of careful groundwork before you can begin a successful programme of communicative teaching. This unit looks at some of the stages along the way, as well as the rewards at the end of this preparatory period.

The students we worked with were in the top stream in an Austrian state school and were in their third year of English. Their classes to date had all been conducted in a very traditional manner. At the beginning of the school year there had been a change of teacher, which presented the new teacher with a whole range of problems arising from differences in approach and method.

The new teacher, the one we worked with throughout this trial unit, had this to say:

From the beginning I had problems because my students were plainly not used to speaking English in class. They had trouble understanding me when I spoke English. Above all it was impossible to get them to speak English with each other or with me. But I noticed that they were fully capable of using English in short role plays and in simulated functional situations like 'asking the way' and 'shopping'. Even their written classwork and homework was OK if they were given clearly delineated tasks such as gap-filling exercises.

But when it came to creative writing, their meagre abilities fell to pieces. They had no faith at all in their ability to produce English. This came out especially in the way they were always reaching for their dictionaries and, as result, any attempt to put their German into English mostly resulted in texts that simply weren't English.

In the light of this assessment and our own observations, we decided to ensure that our approach would give every student some means of relating to the topic of 'Young people and pets'. This meant that a narrow focus on particular language or functional points could not be foremost in our planning. Instead, we chose the broader objectives of (1) raising our students' interest in English in general, and (2) improving the relationship between the students and their teacher. We decided that in order to achieve this we needed (3) to create a learning atmosphere that was as relaxed as possible, and (4) to improve both the students' listening comprehension and their ability to participate in simple interactions in English. We hoped that when this groundwork had been laid, our students could begin to draw on their passive knowledge of English. This, we were sure, must be considerable even if it was almost entirely dormant and unrecognised.

The first step towards achieving these objectives was a phase of preparation for communicative learning. This lasted about ten hours and included:

- Activities for the creation of a low-anxiety environment as in, for example, Brandes and Phillips 1977, Canfield and Wells 1976, Lee 1979, Legutke and Thomas 1991 and Moskowitz 1978.
- Standard task-listening exercises as in, for example, Blundell and Stokes 1981.
- Conventional communicative activities with clear frameworks, clear tasks, and integration of skills. An important step here was the first use of pair and groupwork.

During this stage we observed the class closely. To make the students more aware of their learning processes and to remove any element of secrecy regarding our presence, we discussed with them, in German, what we had been noticing in the class up to that time.

Here is what the group's regular teacher had to say about the situation at the end of this stage:

I have to say that the situation in the class rather quickly and dramatically improved. You can actually feel how the students enjoy the lessons now. They've begun to have fun. They've realised that they can express things in the foreign language, things they really want to say, really want to write, and that they are taken seriously.

There have been some problems. There were, for example, two boys in the class who quite obviously did not want to go along with others. They spent most of the time just sitting either doing absolutely nothing or sniggering and making faces. And I confess that this made me both angry and anxious because I couldn't get them to tell me why they wouldn't cooperate. I began to look for the cause of the problem in myself. The talks in German were especially important. For one thing, during these talks I was able to present certain bits of English interaction language like Pardon?, Excuse me, could you say that again?, Would you spell that word, please?, What's ' . . . ' in German/English? *In addition, students quite soon began to talk about their problems when they noticed that they could do this and get a sympathetic hearing. Most interestingly, the students all say that they've learned quite a lot in the last few weeks and that they can express themselves in English much better now.*

It was against this background and rationale that we began to introduce our model unit, *Young people and pets*.

UNIT SUMMARY
Lesson 1

1 Moving towards more effective groupwork
The students match pictures of children with pictures of different homes. Then they match pictures of animals with the children and their homes.

2 Rapport: bridging the gap between teacher and students
A hand-out guides speculation about the teacher's home and possible pets.

3 Interviewing the teacher
Students ask the teacher questions and compare his or her answers with their guesses.

Lesson 2

4 Pooling and analysing reasons for keeping pets
Students think of and note down reasons for keeping or not keeping a pet.

5 Dialogue building
In pairs, students build dialogues from their pro and con notes, possibly using supplementary language provided in substitution tables.

Lesson 3

6 Personalisation
In pairs, students ask each other about having or not having a pet.

7 Guessing about someone else
Pairwork: everyone notes down clues that they think suggest why their partner does or doesn't have a pet. Partner A with eyes closed, listens to Partner B's 'rationales'. A and B then swap roles.

8 Meta-discussion
A discussion of Stage 7.

Lesson 4

9 Content-oriented groupwork: preparing for role plays
Groups discuss pets and compose group reports based on a model text. Each group chooses another group to read out their report.

10 Role plays
The group reports provide the setting, roles, and dynamics for role plays.

11 Content and process evaluation
A discussion of Stage 10 to raise important points about content and group interaction.

Lesson 5

12 Reflection
The students look at drawings of animals, close their eyes, and think of situations in their lives where they are involved with these animals.

13 Pair/group discussion of feelings
Students record the strengths of their likes and dislikes of these animals by drawing symbols (e.g. a heart) on a hand-out, and then discuss their likes and dislikes in pairs or group.

14 Reflection

Students discuss in pairs how they would react in encounters with different animals.

Lesson 6

15 Discussing beliefs and feelings

Class and teacher discuss received attitudes and biases.

16 Poster presentation

Students create posters on this theme and display them in class.

Preparation

At the beginning of the unit ask students to bring from home any photos or drawings they may have of current or former pets. Keep these in a safe place until needed at Stage 9.

1 Moving towards more effective groupwork

The teacher began by asking the students to work in groups and to match the young people on the poster (see Fig. 1.1 for an example) with the pets and homes. This placed them in a situation which encouraged them not only to justify their decisions but also to use the language of argument: *Yes, but . . . / It can't . . . because . . . / There isn't enough . . ., so . . .*

Where do they live?
What pets have they got?

Jill

Gerry

Dog

Tower block

Horse

Farmhouse

Budgie

Barbara

Cottage

The aim was to give the students experience in the process of reaching group decisions. The rightness or wrongness of their solutions was not a consideration. We did not expect them to speak English right away. We took it for granted that the groups would only gradually develop a way of negotiating decisions and expected that the students would find listening as difficult as speaking.

It is a good idea in weaker groups to present important formulae, or structures, on a poster or on the board. Even so, some groups will have trouble negotiating a decision either because the task is unfamiliar, or because they make no attempt to form a consensus. An option at this point is to remind the group that (a) the two questions of 'Who lives where?' and 'What pets have they got?' need to be discussed as separate issues, and (b) that everyone in the group must agree before they can record their decision.

The process of reaching a group decision did not go well in every group. Given what we knew about the class this was no surprise, and we had agreed beforehand with the teacher that he would, as inconspicuously as possible, take notes on student behaviour. What we wanted was a simple account of who was doing what, to help us learn more about the class dynamic.

In fact the teacher went further and his account turned out to be quite revealing. Here is how he summarised his notes after the lesson.

What surprised me most was how well the group work went, for the most part. I left it up to the students how they should arrange themselves. But then there were problems again with K and T who made a point of showing their unwillingness to work with two girls who were also alone. Due to pressure of time I didn't want to try to deal with the problem then and there so I just put the four of them in a group. The result was, though, that all four of them spoke nothing but German and the two boys were repeatedly disruptive and conspicuously troublesome. I moved from group to group trying to hear as much as I could without breaking in. One thing I noticed was that three of the five groups carried on their discussion almost completely in English. The other two groups generally spoke German but changed to English as I approached.

About five minutes before the end of the lesson it seemed to me that my plan to share my observations with my class was still a good idea. We had just finished comparing the results of the groupwork. During the groupwork phase I had time not only to note down observations but also to think about the form of my feedback. I sat on a table in the middle of the class and looked around. What I said [in German] was something like this: 'I tried today to note down a few thoughts that came to me while you were doing groupwork. I'd like to read them to you now and hope that you will think about it. I don't want to single anyone out for praise or criticism because I don't think it would be a good idea to talk about things like that today. We could do that later if you want.' I could see the curiosity in their eyes but waited a while, feeling that the growing silence was a good sign. Then I began to read. I was so tense that at first my voice quavered.

'Scene 1: I ask you to form groups. I am pleased this happens quite smoothly. Two boys and two girls, however, are still alone. And when I ask them to form a group I notice that the two boys are not too happy about this. Although they don't say anything to me, their manner and certain muttered remarks, doubtless hurtful to the two girls, betray their unwillingness. I wonder how we can get to the point where we can all accept each other.'

A look around the circle of students tells me that my words have had some effect. The students look thoughtful. Some are looking at me, others have their heads down. I continue.

'Scene 2: During the group phase three groups speak practically nothing but English. I can tell by the expressions on their members' faces that they are really involved and enjoy expressing themselves in English. One group is speaking German. When I approach, they all look uneasy and quickly say something in English. Apparently, the English lasts only as long as I am nearby. I wonder how we can get to the point where we are all speak English, even when I am not around like some sort of inspector. Even if it is very difficult at the beginning.'

This was the end of the first lesson. It seemed that it was, after all, possible for a communicative activity to capture the attention of most of the members of the class provided the task was sufficiently clearly structured. As for the few exceptions, the teacher did not straightaway try to stop them using German. Instead, he tried to observe and take notes on what was happening around him as carefully as he could. Reading these observations back to the class enabled him to express his view of how things had gone. It seemed as well that the class could sense their teacher's commitment to the new approach. For the moment, this seemed enough. However, as a class becomes accustomed to thinking about such process issues, they will respond more and more readily to invitations to come in with comments of their own. Eventually, full-scale meta-discussions in which the consequences of this or that feature of instruction process or group interaction can become a feature of every unit.

2 Rapport: bridging the gap between teacher and students

How well the students already know a teacher may depend on the location of the school. Since our school is in a large city, the students in the trial knew little about their teacher. In order to increase the rapport between them and the teacher we decided to make them better acquainted with him. First, he asked his students to note down their preconceptions about him – where he lived, his hobbies and interests, his life-style, etc. This they did mostly in the framework of the hand-out shown in Figure 1.2. Figure 1.3 is an example of one student's notes. (We do not normally collect students' notes of this sort, but in this lesson we did, by prior agreement with the students.)

- Do you think . . .   . . . your teacher has a pet?

  YES   NO

  What do you think?   What do you think?
  Which pet has he got?   Which pet would he like?

- Make notes . . .   . . . about where you think he lives and about his lifestyle
                                            (e.g.: sort of house, flat, room, small garden . . .)

- **Then ask your teacher:**   Make notes:
  - Have you got . . .?
  - Which pet would . . .?
  - Where do you . . .?
  - Have you got a . . .?
  - Do you like . . .?
  - . . .?

Figure 1.2

yes no

dog + cat
I think he lives in a bungalow. 15 rooms,
~~small garden~~, ~~big terrace~~, big garden,
~~big garage~~

Figure 1.3

3 Interviewing the teacher

The first few student questions were prompted by the notes on the hand-outs. Then the students independently decided to find out more about their teacher by writing down further questions. Here, in corrected form, are some of their questions:

Are you married?
Have you got children?
Do you often have problems with your children?
Do your children speak English?
What are your hobbies?
What kind of music do you like?
What would you say if your children wanted to have an expensive pet?

Then the students read out their questions in turn, and were answered by the teacher. The students took notes of his answers and compared them with their guesses.

4 Pooling and analysing reasons for keeping pets

In order to elicit possible reasons for keeping a pet and in order to refer back to the students' discussion of young people and pets in the previous lesson, the teacher wrote the following on the board and asked the students to comment on it:

John Taylor, 13, f, L
+: s, fb, p
−: s, s, c
problem: dog

He then asked, 'What does all this tell us about John?'

The students first speculated about the meanings of the various notes and symbols and then went on to build a story orally, reformulated as follows:

John Taylor is thirteen years old. He lives in a flat in London. He likes sports and he plays football. He does not like school. Perhaps it's boring for him or he is bad at school. He hates spinach. He is fond of pets, but he doesn't like cats. He has a problem because he wants to have a dog. But his parents don't allow that.

In pairs, the students then noted down various reasons why someone might or might not want to have a dog. After a few minutes the teacher elicited these and wrote them on the board as they arose. For homework the students were asked to write down reasons for and against keeping some other sort of pet. Figure 1.4 shows what one student wrote about keeping a parrot.

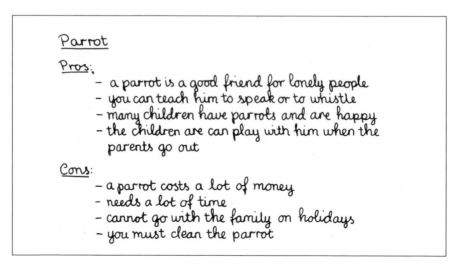

Figure 1.4

5 Dialogue building

The next step was to use the pro and con notes (e.g. Fig. 1.4), along with the language of argument from Stage 1, as raw material in dialogue building. This recycling of language patterns increased students' accuracy, and the highlighting of these particular patterns drew students' attention to the existence of viewpoints different from their own. This paved the way for the role play in Stage 10. Figure 1.5 is an example of one pair's (uncorrected) dialogue.

Keeping a dog

A: I think the dog is a very god guard for the house and the family.
B: I don't think so. Because the dog needs a lot of space.
A: We had a big house and it is not a problem.
B: A dog is very expensive and his food too.
A: It's not true. The dog eats the leftovers.
B: That's right. But a dog needs somebody to look after him and in the holidays he cannot go with the family.
A: The dog can go with me or he is alone and guards the house.
B: The dog tears things.
A: Yes, a young dog, ~~because~~ but he can learn it when he is older.
B: O.K., that's right.

Figure 1.5

This is how these dialogues were actually built:
a The teacher asked pairs to imagine that two people (one pro, the other con) were talking about a pet. Each pair was to agree on which pet the people in their dialogue would talk about.
b The students wrote the dialogue with the teacher walking round and helping out with language.
c When the pairs had finished their dialogues, they were asked, in turn, to come up front and act them out from memory.

Comments: We often find that it is more difficult for students to read dialogues out loud than act them out. Additionally, it is often a good idea to have everyone move to a new seat away from their partner. Otherwise pairs often continue rehearsing or trying to finish their dialogues while the first pairs are 'on stage'.

6 Personalisation

This stage only lasted three or four minutes, with the learners asking each other questions like *Have you got a pet? What is it? What do you call it? How old is it? How big is it? What colour is it? Where does it live? What does it eat?*

Beforehand, the teacher had pointed out the following:

- If someone answered 'No', there should be no further questions.
- They should not go into detail about *why* they had a pet since this would be dealt with in the next stage.

7 Guessing about someone else

After re-eliciting the various pros and cons that came up in Stage 4, the teacher asked the students to note down clues which suggested why their partners did or didn't have a pet and, after that, to note down their own reasons for having or not having a pet. To keep students from looking at their partner's notes, the teacher stressed that their notes were going to be used as the basis for the following activity.

Then Partner A, with eyes closed, listened to Partner B *slowly* read out their guesses about A's reasons for keeping a pet.

The rationale for asking speakers to speak slowly and listeners to sit with eyes closed is as follows:

- It is important for the listeners to hear everything clearly.
- With eyes closed, listeners seem more likely to notice and reflect on what they hear about themselves.

All this creates a good basis for students to realise:

- when they hear an accurate guess
- that they are participating in real communication in a foreign language.

And moments like this may well do more than anything else to stimulate interest in learning English.

Figure 1.6 shows one pair's notes about why one of them, Markus, hasn't got a pet.

Figure 1.6

My partner Markus, have'nt got a pet. He can't say so right if he would like a pet. I think he have'nt a pet, because he don't like it. It isn't important for him, I think — I think he don't like the work with the pet.

> *Why have I not got a pet?*
> *My parents do not like animals in the flat.*
> *The animals need some time and a space.*
>
> *Why do I want a pet?*
> *I like animals. I would like to have a pet, because my parents say not.*

The notes clearly show the difference between how Markus sees his own situation and how his partner imagines it. Whereas Markus would indeed like to have a pet but cannot because his parents object, his partner thinks he is indifferent and does not want to do the work involved in keeping one. In our experience, students frequently do not know such details about each other, despite spending considerable time together in school. Consequently, there is much more potential for information exchange in simple activities like this than one might think.

8 Meta-discussion

In this stage, class and teacher reviewed their experiences in the previous stage.

The teacher simply asked the students to lay their notes out on their tables so that everyone could stroll around, read them and recall their earlier thoughts and feelings.

Following this 'read-walk-read-walk' phase, the teacher brought the whole class together and elicited reasons why people had guessed right and wrong. Was there some basis for inference? Or were guesses simply guesses? This meta-discussion phase (conducted in German) raised a number of interesting issues. For example, the teacher referred back to the eyes-closed listening activity in order to find out the students' reactions to it and to make them aware of the importance of concentration. Here is an extract from the meta-discussion:

Student 1 *What happened with us was that we had written exactly the same things, B and me.*

Teacher . *Really?*

Student 2 *I didn't open my eyes though. It's interesting when you've got your eyes closed. You're in suspense about what your partner thinks of you.*

Student 3 *For me it was like telepathy.*

Teacher   *Did you and your partner have the same thing for everything?*

Student 3   *Yes, partly.*

Teacher   *Could you speak up a bit please?*

Student 3   *I mean, we had a lot of the same things because we know each other really well. T often comes around to my place, but I had the feeling anyway that it was like my partner could read my mind. But we didn't have as much the same as [S1 and S2] did.*

Student 4   *Yes, but we got some things right, even though we don't know each other so well.*

Student 5   *Hm. Yes . . . I just tried to imagine I was you and so some of my guesses were right.*

Teacher   *Could you try to think back to when I asked you to close your eyes? What did you think of that?*

Student 2   *It helped – I was really able to relax that way.*

Teacher   *Do you mean you became somehow calmer?*

Student 6   *It was the same for me, but somehow I kept wondering what my partner thought or didn't think about me.*

Teacher   *That means you started to think about yourself?*

Student 6   *Yes, but I didn't really have enough time for that. When I started to concentrate, you wanted us to do something else again and for that I had to make some notes.*

Teacher   *I see. Sorry, I didn't notice you hadn't finished.*

Student 7   *With us it was like this: I was so curious about what M would write that I couldn't concentrate at all on what I thought about him.*

Teacher   *I was a little bit afraid of that . . . since we don't know each other very well that you might think it was a bit silly my asking you to close your eyes but then I didn't have the impression that . . .*

Student 5   *I found it really nice, so different.*

Teacher   *What do you mean, different?*

Student 5   *I was able to give all my attention to listen to J . . . aside from that I'm not sure.*

Teacher   *J's voice?*

Student 5   *Yes, right. J's voice too. Other times you never listen so consciously to people.*

Student 8   *I noticed that for the first time I didn't even want to try to speak German. Normally when I am looking at who I am talking to I always automatically speak German even though I don't like to. Maybe because we always speak German everywhere else, during break for example.*

Teacher   *Then let's always sit around with our eyes closed. (laughter)*

Teacher   *Did any pair actually speak German during this phase?*

Students   *No. (to each other)*

Student 9   *Last time I even kept speaking English after the lesson, even during the break. I didn't even notice.*

Student 7   *Last time we even spoke to each other in English all during volleyball. I hadn't thought I'd be able to.*

Meta-discussions of this kind give the teacher the chance to discover how the students experienced a certain exercise or teaching phase and what problems they encountered. They help learners become aware of how different individuals react to the same task. This helps to develop empathy; that is, it fosters their ability to put themselves into other people's shoes, a vital social skill. Meta-discussions also play a role in raising awareness of learning processes, as can be seen in the part where Student 8 stated that he had noticed for the first time he had not even wanted to try to speak German. Growth in awareness of ways and stages in learning is essential if students are to come to feel responsible for their own learning.

9 Content-oriented groupwork: preparing for role plays

The teacher brought out the pictures and photos the students had brought in at the beginning of the unit. The students formed groups, showed each other their materials and talked about themselves and their pets: reasons for having or not having them, their attitudes to pets, their problems with pets or with getting pets, and so forth.

After this discussion each group wrote a report on their findings about each other (number of students, pets, opinions, etc.). The teacher encouraged everyone to supplement their reports with visuals. An example text presented on an OHP transparency served as a model for these reports (see Fig. 1.7).

Report (Group A)

2 boys and 2 girls in our group have pets. Petra can't have a pet because her parents say 'no'. They live in a small flat. But she would like to have a little hamster. Her parents are very stict. Tom doesn't want a pet. He thinks pets are disgutsting. All the others think this is not right.

Figure 1.7

As each group finished its report, they exchanged it with another group for silent reading. This was to underline the communicative character of the writing. In order to increase the motivation to produce good, readable reports, the teacher took care to say in advance that they would be shared.

Comment: If possible, in activities like this, each group should be able to decide which other group will read and react to their report. In this class the groups made their choice in the light of the questions:
- Which group knows the least about us as a group?
- Which has a different view of us as a group?

The text produced in the trial class (Fig. 1.8) is a clear example of the degree to which the discussions, as well as the written reports, were rooted in the students' everyday lives. In our experience, such anchoring in reality is essential for many classroom activities to work at their potential best by functioning not only as language learning activities but also as social events. This is particularly true of role plays, which were the next stage of the unit.

Two boys in our group have a dog. The other haven't a pet, but they want a pet. Vikis dog is small and lazy and has black long ears. Robert has a very big dog with black long hair. Wolf want a cat. But his father is strikt, therefore Wolf is sad. Berty want a dog, but his grandma is ill and a dog is too loud for she.

Figure 1.8

10 Role plays

Each group now read the group report they had been given and from it derived the framework for a role play. Here is an example of such a framework, based on the report in Figure 1.7.

Setting: *At the breakfast table in Petra's family*
Roles: *Petra, her parents, her grandmother*
Dynamic: *Petra wants a pet, members of the family argue for and against*

After a very brief discussion period (kept short to prevent participants from trying to remember lines word for word), each group performed their role play in front of the whole class. The amount of content and language brought out earlier in the unit enabled each player to participate realistically in the discussion.

11 Content and process evaluation

This is what the teacher had to say about Stage 10:

It was fascinating to observe how the role players identified with the parts they had taken on. The way they spoke, their faces, their movements – everything was so real it almost seemed it was being said in earnest and had not sprung from what had gone on before in the classroom. Also, all the students paid attention to each other. This probably had to do with the fact that they were not playing just any roles but were always speaking for members of their own group.

Such feelings also came out clearly in the lively discussion following the role play, the first part of which was in English. Again the importance of the links with the students' everyday lives was evident. This extract is from the later phase of the meta-discussion which took place in German.

Student 1   *So, my mother too, always says exactly what J did when she said 'When I was young I couldn't have a pet' and so on.*

Student 2   *J was playing me and what she said is really true. That was exactly my situation she acted out.*

Teacher   *But your mother probably has reasons for being against you having a pet, doesn't she?*

Student 2   *Yes, and she played that too. That I don't always want to clean out the cage . . . I can't really imagine that I'd always do that myself . . .*

12 Reflection

The teacher next asked the students to think about the lives of the animals shown in Figure 1.9. The aim was to evoke other related experiences and memories to stimulate vocabulary recall and generally get the students more involved. To increase concentration, the teacher asked the students first to look closely at each picture, then to close their eyes and think for a full minute. This silent reflection time is *not* a mere embellishment but an important element in the preparation for the next activity.

Figure 1.9

13 Pair/group discussion of feelings

The teacher asked everyone to express the strength of their likes and dislikes by drawing a heart, star and other symbols in the boxes under the pictures in Figure 1.9 (these symbols were the same as those in

Fig. 1.10). Then, after giving out the hand-out shown in Figure 1.10 the teacher asked students to form pairs or small groups and discuss each other's strengths of feeling about the animals.

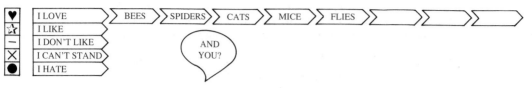

Figure 1.10

14 Reflection

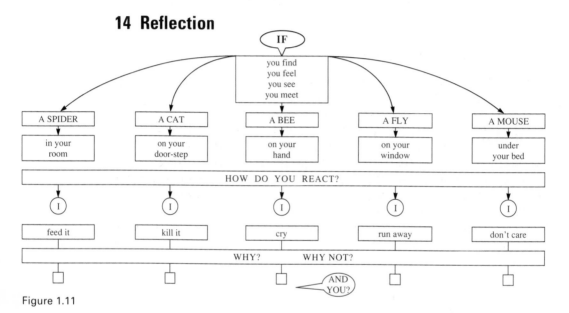

Figure 1.11

After a few minutes, the teacher handed out a copy of Figure 1.11 to each student. He gave the class a minute or so to try to understand how to read it, afterwards inviting suggestions and asking checking questions to ensure that everyone understood how to interpret it. Then, everyone had a few more minutes to fill it out. In the teacher's words:

I asked everyone to stand, mill about and find out how several others would react. Having filled out a worksheet myself, I participated in this phase too, in order to see how they got on. It struck me in the first minutes that I had perhaps not explained clearly enough how the input prompts from the worksheets were to be used, so I interrupted the activity to point out the use of the word if. After that things began to go well with everyone participating in a very lively fashion although I noticed that the students were not always able to express themselves in English. I noted, for example, the following exchange:

Student 1 *If you find a spider in your hand, how do you react?*
Student 2 *I don't kill it. I feed it.*

Student 1 *You feed it? No!*
Student 2 *Yes, I feed it.*
Student 1 *(in German) You can't mean that, you can't tell me that . . .*

Afterwards, I told the class that I thought the activity hadn't gone at all well, because of all the lapses into German, but several students quickly pointed out that part of the instructions on the (original) worksheet had been in German too.

The moral here seems to be that while use of the mother tongue is sometimes unavoidable for vital communicative needs to be met, overuse of the mother tongue by the teacher can be quite counter-productive at other times. If at all in doubt about which language to use, we try to use the target language.

15 Discussing beliefs and feelings

In the trial class, the teacher first presented various stimuli on posters (e.g. Figs. 1.12 and 1.13). These were intended to involve the students in a discussion of their attitudes to certain animals.

The teacher tried to make sure that everybody understood the posters and then allowed a few minutes for students to think and note down their ideas. Finally, he elicited their reactions to the stimulus statements, encouraging them to use language presented on the posters if they wished. Some students recounted their experiences with animals. Stories came up about stray pets, animals being tormented and conflict encounters with animals (one girl had been bitten by a dog). Everything was in English.

Figure 1.12

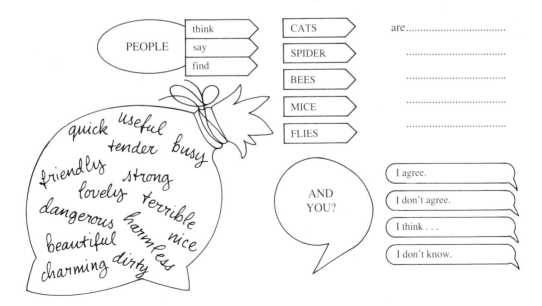

DO YOU AGREE?
If not, write down what you think:

	YES	NO
● Spiders have no right to live.		
● Cats never kill other animals.		
● Flies also want to live.		
● The bee is man's enemy.		
● A mouse cannot be a pet.		

Figure 1.13

The teacher then asked the students to write down their thoughts on the whole unit up to this point. Here are some of their thoughts:

- *We really learnt to use the foreign language, and it was a lot easier than we thought.*
- *It's fun to try to speak only English.*
- *We sometimes 'forgot' about the situation. Speaking English seemed natural towards the end of the unit.*
- *The atmosphere in class improved a lot. We now know each other and our teacher better.*
- *We have lost our fear. We always knew that our English was full of mistakes, but we don't worry about it too much any more.*

> I think it was very good, that we took this topic, because it's interesting to see what other pupils think about pets.
> Everybody thinks spiders are ugly othes find spiders are lovely. And so we learn too see what is in others mind. I like this topic because I like all stories.

16 Poster presentation

This unit was rounded off by making and displaying posters on the theme of young people and pets. This final stage involved students viewing and discussing each others' work – a free speaking activity that offered students the opportunity to practise both the language and the social skills that had been emphasised over the course of the unit.

RETROSPECTIVE

These were the teacher's main comments just after the close of the unit:

- *I hadn't thought I'd be able to pick up this approach so quickly.*
- *I am now very much aware that the social aspects of learning a foreign language are at least as important as the purely linguistic ones.*
- *I think one of the most important conclusions I have drawn from the experience is that it is very important for me as a teacher to stay consistent with my aims. I think, in the past, I always gave up too early.*
- *I will definitely go on teaching in this way. I think I now have ideas I can use to make my lessons more motivating both for me and my students.*

And these were his comments at the end of the school year:

A lot has changed in my teaching since I first started to try these ideas out. I think I have become more aware of what is going on under the surface. I tend to think more in terms of teaching English as an opportunity for real communication that involves my students personally. It also involves me personally a lot and I think it's an ongoing process. I am now thinking a lot more about my own role as a teacher, I am more aware of when and how I want to take responsibility for the learning process of my students and when and how I want to shift responsibility from myself to my learners. I have also gone through phases of doubt since I started to change my teaching – at various points I was worried about the fact that my students made so many mistakes, but it just showed me that in my previous teaching I had not given my learners enough opportunity to use English for real communication and therefore I had never got a picture of their real language level. Another thing that was necessary was to point out to my students that the fact that the lessons had become more fun did not mean that everything else had to change somehow too. It is still important for them to learn vocabulary, for example, prepare for tests, bring their home assignments and so on and so forth.

One thing strikes me: teaching in this way means a lot of work, but when I leave a class at the end of a lesson I nearly always feel that my energy level is higher than it was before I went in. So in a way I feel I get more than I give.

Nightmare

Students on their way to cooperative learning

LEVEL

Lower intermediate +

TIME

2–3 hours

TRIAL CLASS

Twenty thirteen- to fourteen-year-olds in their fourth year of English; three fifty-minute lessons a week

AIMS

Building basic social skills; encouraging students to act independently but with a sense of responsibility; diminishing students' feelings of linguistic inadequacy; encouraging students to speak about their own lives and experience; introducing students to the evaluation of student–student interaction; contextualising, rehearsing and managing role plays and exploiting them in further work

Language areas and skills

Oral fluency; listening; writing; reading; practice of language for expressing/advocating decisions

Materials

Stage 1: Picture for brainstorming (optional), (Fig. 2.1, p. 29)
Stage 2: Hand-out of reading text ('Nightmare', p. 30)
Stage 3: Poster or OHP transparency of word list (Fig. 2.2, p. 31)
Stage 5: Hand-out of picture with blank speech bubbles (Fig. 2.3, p. 32)
Stage 6: Observation sheet (Fig. 2.4, p. 33)
Stage 9: Model mini-text (optional), (p. 36)
Stage 10: Photos, pictures, magazines, newspapers, felt-tip pens, scissors, glue, large sheets of paper for making collage

BACKGROUND AND RATIONALE

Social skills learned in the language classroom can be of value in students' relations with people in general. An example from our experience springs to mind:

In the mid-1970s I (HP) had a class of lower stream twelve-year-old boys. I tried a milling activity with them. I asked the boys to stand up, walk around, mingle and briefly interview several classmates in turn. They were rowdy and the activity was plainly failing. After a few minutes I broke it off and asked the boys to sit with me in a circle. I asked them how they had felt during the activity, trying to find out why they had behaved as they had. Interestingly, they began by complaining about each other, about how the others had been too noisy and how they had been jostled, bumped into and otherwise distracted. A typical complaint ran like this: 'Hannes came up to ask me a question, but started by elbowing me. This made me angry. And this kind of thing kept happening.' I pointed out to them that if an English-speaking person wants to attract someone's attention they do so by saying 'Excuse me'. I wrote *Excuse me* on the board and before the next milling phase I reminded them that this was what they should say when they wanted to attract someone's attention. And in fact during the second milling phase the boys were very careful to do this, to use the words *Excuse me*. The activity worked quite well despite the fact that these same boys, when talking to each other in their mother tongue during class breaks actually did jostle each other in just the way that had made them so angry during the first milling phase.

This example shows one way in which the foreign language class can become an arena for the development of a basic element of cooperative behaviour, in this case, appropriate use of a polite phrase. Of course, the newly learnt behaviour will not automatically transfer into the learners' everyday behaviour. On the other hand, we have seen many clear examples of this happening. Besides, what is the alternative to trying?

UNIT SUMMARY

Lesson 1

1 Brainstorming
Use a picture of somebody asleep in bed to activate students' associations.

2 Reading
Students read the text ('Nightmare').

3 Getting the students to talk
Present a word list on an OHP transparency, poster or the board. Students select three words and link them orally in a sentence or two to explain the situation described in the text.

4 Analysis of the associations

Remove the word list. The students offer their own interpretations of the situation in the text.

Lesson 2

5 Dialogue building

Students work in pairs to create a dialogue. Each student takes one of the roles given in the text.

6 Role play rehearsal

Students get together in groups of four. Within the foursomes, first one pair and then the other act out their role play with the other pair observing. Guided by an observation sheet, the observing pair evaluates the role play of the other pair.

7 Reaching a decision about the role plays

Each group decides which pair will act out their role play in front of the whole class. This decision is based on evaluation and feedback stimulated by the observation sheet.

Lesson 3

8 Role plays

Students present their role plays to the whole class.

9 Writing mini-texts

Either present text lead-ins or hand out a model text to guide students in producing mini-texts of their own. Students read out their texts to the class.

10 Error correction and text collage

Students publish their texts as collages of mini-texts, drawings, photos, newspaper clippings and whatever else.

1 Brainstorming

Brainstorming is a familiar technique for eliciting and, to a certain extent, presenting vocabulary on a given theme. It is also useful for stimulating interest in a theme for its own sake. (See De Bono 1970 for a discussion of brainstorming in creative thinking.)

A typical brainstorming begins with the teacher writing a word or phrase on the board, or by showing a picture or, as in this case, by drawing one.

You can then ask the students to call out any word associated with the prompt *as soon as* it occurs to them and without worrying about how it is linked to the prompt. You, or one or more of the students, write the elicited vocabulary on the board as quickly as possible and with no criticism or correction *whatever*. When you have a fair number of words on the board, there are many ways to proceed. Just to give two examples:

1 Invite students, individually, in pairs or in small groups, to write the words down on a sheet of paper in categories which they then explain and justify to the rest of the class.
2 Rub out all the words and then ask the class to try to recall them. As you re-elicit the vocabulary, you can rewrite it (including corrections of spelling and so on) in a way that demonstrates the connections between words.

For the trial class, we chose a third option. To help trigger off the brainstorming we planned for the teacher to draw the figure of someone asleep in bed (Fig. 2.1) which would lead into the text 'Nightmare' in Stage 2. This was done on a large sheet of paper with about 15 cm along the right edge folded back to hide the words the teacher had written there earlier (see Fig. 2.2 on p. 31).

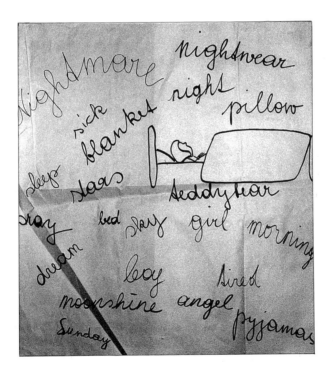

Figure 2.1
This is what the students in our class wrote with no other prompt than the picture shown. (They were already used to such free association work)

Usually, for a brainstorming like this to succeed with an inexperienced class, the teacher needs to assume the role of facilitator. Here is an example from another class of how this can work:

Teacher *Look here! (while beginning to draw the picture) What is it?*
Student *It's a bed.*
Teacher *What do you think of when you see a bed?*
Student *Sleep.*
Teacher *OK.* Sleep *for example. Why don't you write down some other words that come to your mind when you think of* bed?

During the eliciting of different associations students learn how the same picture can stimulate different interpretations. This is no small or obvious thing. If the growth of cooperative independent learning is your aim, then it is essential first of all that students become aware that different people have different perceptions. However, the demands of a brainstorming phase may well exceed students' ability to express themselves in the foreign language. So you may need to supply, among other things, the interaction language necessary if students are to be able to work together in English. That is, expressions such as *What does '. . .' mean? What do we do now?* or *What was that again?*

2 Reading

In foreign language teaching, texts are very often used only at the cognitive level, with affective considerations being neglected. That is, some teachers view texts purely as a means of presenting or practising target structures or vocabulary rather than as stimuli that get the learners personally involved. In the trial class, when we asked students to read the text our aim was to exploit the *affective* potential of our text by showing how it could have quite different interpretations for different people. The text we used was as follows:

Nightmare

In the middle of the night Charlie woke up. At first he lay there, listening, half-asleep. He wasn't really sure what it was. Sometimes it was far away; sometimes it was near – that was what had woken him. And occasionally it was very near indeed. Now he was really awake.

Charlie pulled the bedclothes over his head. Now he could hear nothing except the sound of his heart beating and his breathing. But he couldn't fall asleep again because he knew it was still there. After a while, the smell of warm bedding, warm pyjamas, and his warm self became too much for him. Suddenly he threw back the covers and sat up in bed.

He couldn't see anything in the darkness, but all of a sudden he cried out loudly. Panic overcame him. After a while, he let his head slip back on the pillow. He wanted to go to sleep again. But he couldn't stop thinking. So he decided to wake up Wilson, his brother, who was sleeping in the next bed.

3 Getting the students to talk

The teacher now unfolded the right flap of the poster to reveal a list of words he had written earlier (as in Fig. 2.2). (These could also be presented on an OHP transparency.)

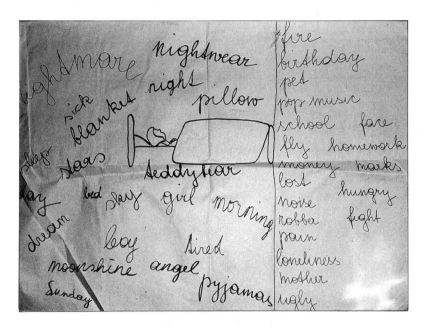

Figure 2.2

By way of example the teacher selected three words – *robber, money, lost* – and said a sentence using these three words: 'Last night I *lost* my *money* because a *robber* came into the hotel.'

He then asked each student to select three words from the list and make up to three sentences speculating about Charlie's situation.

Here is an uncorrected transcript of part of this stage:

Teacher   *Pick out three words to explain Charlie's worries.*
Student 1   *Fire – birthday – pain.*
Teacher   *What do you mean by that?*
Student 1   *I think Charlie had birthday and he went up. Suddenly he saw a great fire and he felt pain.*
Teacher   *Did he get into the fire?*
Student 1   *Yes.*
Student 2   *Mother – marks – homework: I think he's got a bad mark for homework and the mother was angry.*
Teacher   *She got angry, I see.*
Student 3   *Ugly – face – robber: I think Charlie dreamt of a robber with an ugly face. And then he woke up because the robber had an ugly face.*
Student 4   *Fight – lost his face: there were two men who hated each other and so they had a fight and the fight was so terrible that one of the men lost his face.*

Teacher   *A very bad dream, wasn't it?*

Student 5   *Charlie – loneliness – mother: Charlie wasn't here and her mother suddenly felt loneliness.*

Student 6   *Flies – school – marks: Charlie got bad marks and he flew from the school.*

Teacher   *Oh, he had to leave school, you mean?*

Student 6   *And his problem was, he had learnt too little.*

Student 7   *Birthday – fire – school: On Charlie's birthday there was a fire in the school. So he dreamt about that.*

Student 8   *Pop music – fire – fly: When he is dancing to pop music his blood gets in the fire he flies in his thoughts away.*

4 Analysis of the associations

The teacher took down the poster, so that the students could not see the column of prompt words, and then asked them to make new sentences about the character in the picture (Charlie) without necessarily using any of the prompt words. Here are some of the students' (uncorrected) interpretations:

Teacher   *What are the problems Charlie might have?*

Student 1   *I think Charlie has quarrelled with his friends.*

Student 2   *I think he had difficulties with his parents.*

Student 3   *I think he had problems with his teacher.*

Student 4   *Perhaps he will get ill.*

Student 5   *I think Charlie has got problems with himself because he's grown up.*

Student 6   *Perhaps he's lost his girlfriend.*

5 Dialogue building

The teacher put the students into pairs and gave each pair a hand-out (Fig. 2.3). They carried on the story from the point where Charlie had woken up his brother Wilson by filling in the speech bubbles.

Figure 2.3

In our class, the activity worked like this: Partner A filled in the first speech bubble for Wilson and then passed the hand-out on to Partner B who filled in the first speech bubble for Charlie. Partner B then passed the hand-out back to Partner A who filled in the second speech bubble for Wilson and so on.

That is, the number of copies equalled the number of student pairs. Another way of doing this activity, which doubles the amount of writing and involvement in the role play for everyone and greatly reduces the amount of time spent waiting for a partner to finish writing, is the 'Two-way Role Play' (Frank and Rinvolucri 1983, p. 118). Each student has a hand-out and everyone begins by filling out the same speech bubble for the same character. Everyone then passes their sheet to the person on their left (for example) and then fills in the first speech bubble for the other role. When they have done this they pass the sheet back to the person they got it from who then fills in the second speech bubble for the first character to speak and so on.

6 Role play rehearsal

The dialogues developed in the writing phase served as a foundation for a role play. The teacher divided the class up into groups of about four. In each group one pair acted out the role play while the other pair observed, with an observation sheet (see Fig. 2.4). After each role play, the group discussed it using the structures provided on the observation sheet. Then the pairs switched roles.

WATCH AND CRITICISE!						
I THINK WE THINK	Werner Susan Peter and Tony ...		was were	not too	aggressive afraid nervous surprised grumpy	enough.
	his her their	English		was was not	good. fluent. OK.	
	his her their	face(s) voice(s)	should should not		be sound look	more less so	grumpy. aggressive. afraid. nervous.

Such observation guidelines not only direct students' attention to the issue of error correction (which may just be a matter of simply imitating the teacher) but also and more importantly, they help students to develop a better awareness of communicatively appropriate expressions. This guidance also helps students to identify with the roles that they are playing. (An evaluative phase further encourages such development.)

Figure 2.4

When organising role plays like this, you will need to ensure that students doing the role plays do not read directly from the hand-outs they filled out in the previous stage since reading out loud typically leads to rather stilted intonation.

You will probably have to adapt the observation task-sheets we used to suit the requirements of your own class. However, the sheets should always include some stimuli to *non-linguistic* evaluation. The observers should watch non-verbal behaviour in the role play, so it might be helpful to draw attention to the importance of body language (mime, gesture, movements, etc.). Some discussion beforehand will, of course, be necessary in the case of students who are not used to evaluating their own and other students' performance in groupwork. Even so, some students find it difficult to participate effectively in such evaluation phases, as we have learned from some teachers who have experimented with this type of activity.

If you want to tackle these issues with your students you need, again, patience and a willingness to discuss things frankly.

7 Reaching a decision about the role plays

Using their observations of the role plays, the groups decided which pair would act out the role play between Charlie and Wilson in front of the whole class. The aim of this decision phase was to help students to develop their ability to evaluate their own performance – an ability which is essential if lessons are to become less teacher-centred without degenerating into chaos.

The following uncorrected transcript shows how much the differing viewpoints of individual students can influence this decision making.

Student 1   *R and K were very good but speaking too fast.*
Teacher   *Yes, we could hardly follow, but it was a very nice dialogue. It was a very good dialogue.*
Student 2   *Was heißt* munter? *[What does* munter *mean?]*
Teacher   *Vivid.*
Student 3   *It was very vivid. They had a very nice dialogue.*
Student 4   *They spoke too fast.*
Teacher   *Yes, I think they were a little bit excited.*
Student 5   *(referring to different group) It was the same with you, wasn't it? S was very nervous . . .*
Student 6   *. . . but her English was very good.*

8 Role plays

This stage, the acting out of the role plays, was a kind of publication of the work done in all the previous stages of the unit. The step-by-step preparation for the final role plays gave the performers ample opportunity to perfect their language and get over much of their stage fright. The thorough preparation also seemed to give the performers the confidence to go beyond their earlier scripts and to include expression of further anxieties, expectations and fantasies.

Given this level of potential personal involvement, it is well worth devoting plenty of attention to staging. Get the audience to sit quite close to the players. Ask the students to scrunch together in a horseshoe around the centre of the action. If it is not possible to move chairs into this arrangement, students can sit on the floor or on their desks. The first time you organise a role play of this sort, include a discussion phase in which you and the students agree on a set of symbols (e.g. ○ or ∩) so that in future lessons, you can minimise pre-performance chaos by simply drawing the appropriate symbol on the board to show the seating arrangement you want. Encourage students to get into position quietly and also remember to positively reinforce instances of cooperation by praising the students involved.

9 Writing mini-texts

It is very likely that students watching the role plays will recall experiences related to the ones they are seeing portrayed. If you observe the role plays, the 'audience' and their reactions carefully, you will find role plays a rich source of stimuli for further work such as text writing. You can capitalise on topics and emotions figuring in the role plays by noting down (on the board, etc.) ad hoc text lead-ins. These are words, phrases or sentences which cry out for completion and elaboration in the form of a story, letter, description, etc., depending on the lead-in you choose.

Some of the text lead-ins used in the trial class were:

When I came home the other day . . .
First I could not believe my eyes!
Last . . .
I was . . .

The students completed these lead-ins individually to produce short pieces of narration, description or evaluation, often showing a high degree of spontaneity and creativity. Because they were short, students were able to produce them in class. Figure 2.5 is an example of one of these mini-texts. (We learned this technique from Hans-Eberhard Piepho.)

Figure 2.5

Last Friday I was watching TV. After half an hour I fell asleep. Suddenly I woke up. What was it? There was a loud noise. I had a look at the other rooms. But I could not see anything. I was really frightened. Suddenly a voise said, "Hands up". I quickly rose my arms and then I heard a shot. But I was still alive. Now I knew - telly was still on.

If your students are not used to writing texts even of this length, you can hand out a *short* model text that they can identify with. For young people, this often means that they can imagine the text having been written by someone of their own age. If you make sure that students study it carefully before beginning to write, working with the model generally results in effective transfer of the overall structure of the text as well as of important bits of language.

Here is a model text we used in a different trial class, together with a piece of student writing based on it (Fig. 2.6).

When I came home the other day, I was very nervous. I'd got a bad result in my test at school. I couldn't tell my parents about it. The following night I had a strange dream. I suddenly woke up. I didn't know where I was. I looked around. It was dark. Somebody was in my room! All my school stuff was lying on the floor. All over it! I heard something. Who was it? I was scared to death . . . I started to shout, but then I found out who it was: Parker, my terrier.

When I came home the other day I was very nervous. I got a bad mark in my test at school and I could not tell my parents about it. The following night I had a strange dream. I went to sleep. When you do not show the test to your parents then comes a big spider and takes you. I got up and said: "This was a ghost, and I was very much afraid of it. I took my test and went with it to my parents and showed my parents. They said, "OKAY but you must learn very much for the next test. Go to sleep. "I said:„ Good night father, Good night mum"
„Good night Sue"

Figure 2.6

A drawback of working from a model text after a role play (instead of from a text lead-in) is that students tend to draw on the text, rather than on their own experience, for content, which lessens their emotional involvement in the writing. The greater the affective depth of the role plays, the greater this disadvantage is likely to be. Text lead-ins, being much less explicit than model texts about overall text structure and language patterns, seem to stimulate rather than restrict creative interest. Even so, if the model text is interesting enough and relates to the students' world of experience, then the resulting mini-texts can still show a good measure of creative involvement.

10 Error correction and text collage

You can deal with written errors in the mini-texts either during the writing or afterwards, as seems best. If you, the student or other students mark corrections on the text, students should rewrite the texts to produce a fair copy. They can then display these or pass them around the class.

In the final lesson of the trial class students produced a text collage consisting of their corrected, rewritten mini-texts and various visuals which they either made or chose. (Suitable visuals can include drawings, photos, pictures from magazines, newspaper clippings and so forth.)

This mode of presenting texts can have a positive effect on learning as it increases student motivation to produce texts of quality for presentation to the class, and for eventual evaluative comment. That is, the collage presentation can lead to a final discussion phase, with teacher and students standing in front of the collage. You can stimulate discussion by asking questions such as: 'Who do you think had the most fearful experience?', etc.

Part of the text collage produced by this class is shown in Figure 2.7.

Figure 2.7

Variation

We hope we have shown here how a particular sequence of activities worked with teenage learners. The individual activities can be adapted to many other topics or used in adult classes too. For example, two of Michael's trainees have adapted part of this sequence of activities to fit the topic of the 'generation gap' in an upper intermediate class.

This is a revised version of their lesson summary:

1 Activation of associations

Present a photograph showing a parent and a child in a confrontational situation. If such a photograph is difficult to get hold of, an alternative is to present the two following sentences in speech bubbles:

'My parents don't understand me at all.'

'When I was young, I knew how to behave.'

2 Brainstorming and discussion

Ask students to call out their associations. Collect them on the board and discuss.

3 Reading

Hand out the extract from *I'm Your Mother* (Collange 1987) given below.

4 Preparation and rehearsal of role plays

Ask students to build a role play as suggested in the unit. Possible roles could be a child and a parent, or two parents, who have just read the extract.

5 Presentation of the role plays

Students act out their role plays with evaluation and comment as suggested above.

Why? For heaven's sake why?

Why can't you ever turn out the light or shut the door when you leave a room?

Why can't you ever put back a dictionary or a telephone book when you've used them?

Why do you always make the pencils, biros and notepads disappear which have been carefully placed by the telephone or in the kitchen to write down important messages or shopping lists?

Why do you never replace the roll of paper without giving a thought to the next occupant of the bathroom?

Why do you throw your jackets or coats on to the furniture instead of putting them on a coathanger? . . .

*After all, you can't say we haven't said, stressed, emphasised, repeated time and time again, in every possible tone of voice: 'Don't forget, put it away'. . . 'PUT IT AWAY. DON'T FORGET . . . 'DON'T FORGET, PUT IT AWAY'. . . **'PUT IT AWAY, DON'T FORGET'. . .***

Of course it's boring tidying up and thinking about possessions, but if you neglect them they get their own back by getting dirty, broken or lost.

As we're not yet living in the robot era when, according to your science-fiction books, these machines will take over everything from us, our manual tasks, our memories, even our brains – I get landed with the things you haven't done. Anything you can't find I have to look for: if it has disappeared, got lost or been stolen I have to replace it.

I'm your mother, not your daily.

I really don't see why I should slog away at tedious little jobs while you lie sprawled on your bed for hours, listening to your music. I'm sick of picking up your things from all over the place, and tired of ironing your shirts because 'You're so good at it, Mum'. I've had enough of taking back the empties to the bottle bank, and of missing the beginning of the TV film because I had to finish tidying up the kitchen. I love idling about too.

Christiane Collange, *I'm Your Mother*, Arrow Books 1987 pp. 45–7

Pressure

An unusual and powerful way to text reception and production

LEVEL
Lower intermediate +

TIME
2–3 hours

TRIAL CLASS
Twenty-seven fourteen-year-olds in their fourth year of English; three fifty-minute lessons a week

AIMS
Creating experiential/emotional reference points prior to reading; raising motivation for reading; sensitising students to feelings expressed or implied in a text; analysing an author's intentions; building affective links between a reading and a writing task

Language areas and skills
Oral fluency; listening; writing; vocabulary keyed to text and topic

Materials
Stage 1: Rope (5–10 m long, depending on class size)
Stage 5: Hand-outs of reading texts with tasks ('Roller Chaos' and 'Normal Event', pp. 46–7)
Stage 8: Blu-tack

BACKGROUND AND RATIONALE

One thing authorities now agree on is that understanding a written (or spoken) text is an active and creative process, in which the reader (or listener) continually tries to make sense of the text in terms of what they already know. In this view, understanding a text according to a writer's (or speaker's) intention is only possible if (at least) part of the writer's and reader's perceptions of reality overlap. Thus, a text describing a cold winter is bound to remain remote in many respects to readers who have lived all their lives in a tropical country. But even if the content of a text is within the *learner* readers' world of experience, we feel it is essential for teachers to help them animate relevant life experience and to guide them in applying this experience in the reading of foreign language texts. In this unit we describe how we tried to make the students' encounter with a potentially difficult authentic reading text as meaningful as possible. Taking a cue from Stevick's (1976) assertion that 'language learning is a total human experience', we decided specifically to support the reading work with a good deal of relevant in-class experience.

UNIT SUMMARY
Lesson 1

1 Activation of experience: 'The Crowd in the Noose'
Students stand together in a group, close their eyes and quietly concentrate on their sensations. Encircle the group with a rope and steadily tighten it.

2 Brainstorming on the board
The students leave the circle and write words for their feelings/associations on the board.

3 Exploration of the experience
The students comment on the words on the board, discuss the pressure situation (Stage 1) and bring in more personal associations.

4 Structuring vocabulary
Structuring and extension of the vocabulary on the board. Using a handout, the students mark emotive words negative or positive, note associations with similar situations, etc.

Lesson 2

5 Reading the texts
Texts: 'Roller Chaos' and 'Normal Event'. Reading tasks: The students match emotive words to situations described in the texts. They reflect on the texts and compare their approach.

6 Follow-on
Discussion of the experiences brought out in Stage 5.

Lesson 3

7 Text production
The students complete text lead-ins displayed on the board or on posters.

8 Text publication
The students' texts are displayed. Everyone circulates freely and reads.

9 Feedback
Each student shares their feelings about their texts with one or more fellow writers.

1 Activation of experience: 'The Crowd in the Noose'

The teacher asked the class to stand within a seven-metre length of rope laid in a large loop on the floor. The teacher grasped both ends of the rope and pulled them together to enclose the group. Without being asked, a couple of students helped the teacher raise the rope, so that it encircled the whole group at waist level. The teacher's voice was calm but definite as he said: 'Would you close your eyes now, please? Whatever you feel or notice now, don't open your eyes. Just concentrate on your feelings. Don't open your eyes.' A few students began to giggle, but suddenly fell silent as the teacher quietly said, 'Try to concentrate on your feelings. Don't open your eyes.' The group remained silent as the teacher tightened the loop, at first just crowding the students a bit closer together but finally pressing them tightly together and pulling them back and forth.

Figure 3.1
The teacher
tightens the rope
around the
students

2 Brainstorming on the board

'Think of one or more words that have to do with your feelings or with the situation here. Then leave the circle and write your words on the board.' Saying this, the teacher gradually loosened the rope and brought the pressure phase to an end. One student after another slipped under the rope, went to the board and wrote *their* word for expressing *their* emotional experience.

3 Exploration of the experience

The teacher asked the students to say something about these words. Asking questions such as *Who wrote . . .? / What do you mean by . . .? / What are the words you know and what are the words you don't know?* the teacher guided this phase and encouraged students to speak. The communicatively natural management of the discussion by the teacher – without error correction – stimulated comment, explanation, elaborations and questions, as we see here:

Teacher   *What about* lovely? *Who wrote that?*
Student 1 *I . . . I had a lovely feeling when we were all so . . .*
Teacher   *. . . together, you mean?*
Student 1 *Yes.*
Teacher   *Interesting. So you did not mind that. Did you all have positive feelings?*
Students   *(some, hesitating) Yes.*
Teacher   *Could you describe your feelings a bit more? Tell me what was positive about them.*
Student 2 *I think we all were one big person. I think. We all were in the circle and the circle was so than a . . . Than a, not a line, a wall round us and, I think, we all like to be in the class and so, we are a big group.*
Teacher   *Fantastic. And who wrote* light?
Student 3 *I.*
Teacher   *What do you mean by that?*
Student 3 *Er . . . when I closed my eyes, I had no feeling of small . . . I was out. I was not in, I mean I was not in the middle of the circle.*
Teacher   *So you didn't feel the pressure so much?*
Student 3 *No.*

The students were thoroughly involved – not just cognitively, but emotionally as well – and had the opportunity to air both positive and negative feelings.

Student 4 *All were in the circle, nobody was out, so I felt very good, all do the same.*
Teacher   *Everyone did the same, mhm.*
Student 4 *We were all friends.*

Teacher	*And when you felt the pressure? When you felt the others pushing? You were so quiet. Was that because of the camera?*
Students	*No.*
Teacher	*Why then?*
Student 5	*I think we know the feeling. Because we all go to school by bus or by tram. So it was nothing . . . I think it was not a new feeling . . . I think it was not a new feeling . . . we all push in the tram and so, it was not new.*
Teacher	*Do you always close your eyes on the tram?*
Students	*(laugh)*
Teacher	*I mean, try to think of the situation once more. When I asked you to close your eyes and when all of a sudden you could feel this pressure . . . and the others close to yourself . . .*
Student 6	*I think it was also a negative feeling because I don't know what would come now and then it was better I knew that I should write down the words on the blackboard . . . Then I felt OK.*
Student 7	*I think you wanted to kill us.*
Teacher	*Really? (laughs)*
Student 7	*No, but I . . . I was a little afraid . . .*

Indeed, activities like 'The Crowd in the Noose' can trigger quite powerful memories:

Student 8	*In the hospital . . . my grandfather was in hospital and there are . . . er . . . sometimes so many people, and have the feeling it's too small.*
Teacher	*Do you mean visitors?*
Student 8	*Yes, visitors and er . . .*
Teacher	*. . . patients.*
Student 8	*Yes, and doctors as well*
Teacher	*But that's bad, isn't it?*
Student 8	*Yes, in the big rooms, there are so many beds with* Patienten *. . .*
Teacher	*. . . patients . . .*
Student 8	*. . . and patients, yes, and there are so many people so when I would like to sleep that's horrible . . . one person to one bed is OK, but not ten to one bed. That's too many.*

This recollection by one student caused others to recall similar experiences:

Student 9	*In the lift there also many people.*
Teacher	*Where?*
Student 9	*In the lift. I think what K said about the hospital. In the hospital are lifts which are big and there are so many people in them and this was the feeling I had last.*
Teacher	*Which you last had here when you were all packed together?*
Student 9	*Yes, when all go to the blackboard.*
Teacher	*Oh, I see. That was like going out of the lift.*
Student 9	*Going out of the lift. And this was the one negative feeling.*

Teacher   *The only negative?*
Student 9 *Yes. The only.*

The teacher elicited further associations and comments by asking questions like:
- Is there any other situation you are reminded of?
- What's positive or negative for you on the board?
- What does the word '. . .' remind you of?
- Did you have any other positive or negative feelings?

etc.

Again, our aim was to evoke a maximum of emotive memories relevant to the topic area in order to make it easier for the students to re-experience the reality behind a text that deals with similar feelings. Our underlying assumption was that the association of emotions and clear images with the words and structures of which the text is composed would greatly facilitate their retention in long-term memory.

4 Structuring vocabulary

Most authorities on vocabulary learning believe that people can learn words faster if they encounter them in arrangements that reflect aspects of their organisation in the minds of native speakers. Figure 3.2 shows how graphics can suggest mental grouping according to positive/negative 'feeling'. Graphic structuring like this also alerts the students to finer details of spelling, collocation and meaning.

In the trial class the teacher rewrote the words that the students had written on the board in different categories and asked the students to think of more words for each category.

Situations

	wedding ceremony		school yard		shop
	party	in the	cinema		factory
at a	pop concert		tram		disco
	bus stop			in a	fight
	ticket office				traffic jam
					queue
at the airport		during rush hour			crowd

Feelings

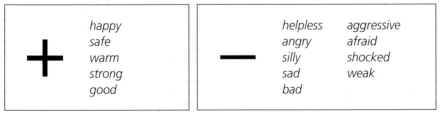

happy		helpless	aggressive
safe		angry	afraid
+ warm		**—** silly	shocked
strong		sad	weak
good		bad	

Figure 3.2

5 Reading the texts

We hoped that the affective (emotional) work done so far would now be of use to the students in their reading of 'Roller Chaos' (Fig. 3.3) and 'Normal Event' (Fig. 3.4).

The teacher began by stressing to the class that during the first reading of each text they should *not* try to understand every word. To make students feel more comfortable with their limited comprehension of the texts in the beginning, the teacher set tasks which concentrated students' attention on those parts of the text where the meaning most important for interpretation is implied rather than stated. The function of the boxes and arrows on Figure 3.3 is to alert students to the presence of such implications.

Accordingly, the tasks were:

a *Read Text 1 and match the following words with the boxes in order to describe the feelings of the people in the various situations:*
helpless helpful angry destructive strong strict weak enthusiastic aggressive sad happy

b *Read Text 2 and find out:*
(i) what the writer of this letter thinks about pop concerts;
(ii) what he thinks about articles like 'Roller Chaos'.

Roller chaos

MELBOURNE — More than 200 girls were treated by ambulance officers at the Bay City Rollers concert in Melbourne last week.

Most were carried sobbing and screaming out of the hall by the officers.

After the show, police called in extra cars when about 300 fans, thinking the group was still at the hall, charged down Rosslyn Street.

Police linked arms along one side of the street while others in a courtesy car appealed to the girls to go home.

When the manager's car arrived, the girls swarmed around it, believing it had come for the group.

Police took over an hour to clear the area after the show had finished.

Bouncers lifted unconscious girls onto the stage and carried them through back doors where a team of St John Ambulance officers were waiting to treat them.

Members of the group and the compere, Ian Meldrum, shouted appeals over the microphones for the girls to keep quiet.

The road behind the hall looked like a battlefield.

Ambulance men and women helpers worked from four vehicles, treating girls who had passed out.

The show was stopped a second time when fans at the rear of the hall pushed forward, crushing those in front against the stage.

Police and officials linked arms but were unable to stop the crowd.

(*Australasian Express*)

Bay City Rollers: a group of pop musicians
sobbing: crying
fans: admirers of the group
linked: joined
swarmed: crowded
bouncers: people responsible for keeping order at dances, pop concerts, etc.
compere: announcer
passed out: fainted

Figure 3.3 Text 1

Michael Swan, *Spectrum*, CUP 1978 p. 10

NORMAL EVENT

Recently I read an article about the behaviour of teenagers at pop concerts. Words like ''uncontrollable,'' and ''dreadful,'' were used to describe the fans' behaviour — but I think this is most unfair.

In my experience, pop concerts have been fantastic; there has never been any trouble or violence, and even though some girls faint, critics don't seem to understand that this is due to pure emotion.

I am sure that a lot of other ''Jackie'' readers feel the same way as I do. So come on, all you critics — pop concerts are normal, enjoyable events and not nearly as terrible as you think!

A Mud Fan,
Skelmersdale,
Lancs.

(Letter in *Jackie*, a girls' magazine)

A Mud Fan: an admirer of the pop group called 'Mud'

Figure 3.4 Text 2
ibid. p.11

The main aim was to encourage students to focus on just those passages in Text 1 which suggest emotional experiences. These occur particularly where the writer of the text describes the emotional and/or physical *pressure* that various people were exposed to. And this is, of course, the reason why, at the beginning of the lesson, the students were physically involved in a pressure experience, for it was in this stage that the teacher prepared the students for the subjective element of the writer's reportage. Working through the specific instances mentioned in the two texts (with several references back to the pressure stage and the subsequent discussion) helped the learners to compare them.

6 Follow-on

In the follow-on work (done in a teacher-led plenary, or whole group session) the students compared the words they had put in the boxes. Here, what was important was not that students had particular right answers but that they explained *why* they had written the words they had. This led into a critical analysis of the intentions of the writers of each of the two texts:

Student 9   *There are two texts. The first is negative and . . .*
Teacher   *What do you mean – 'negative'?*
Student 9   *This newspaper writes negative about the pop concert. They . . .*
Teacher   *How can you say that they write negatively?*
Student 9   *They say most were carried out screaming and sobbing. That means that they were very aggressive.*
Teacher   *Aha. Let me just write down another word (writes* aggressive *on the board). I see your point. And I think there's something else that tells you perhaps that they write negatively about the pop concert.*
Student 3   *Sure. The 'Roller Chaos'.*
Teacher   *Pardon?*

Student 3   *'Chaos.'*
Teacher   *Ah, chaos. Yes.*
Student 4   *Police was helpless. They could not do anything.*
Teacher   *(writes new words on the board) Helpless, chaos. And what about the next text?*
Student 1   *I think this was a pop fan and he writes to a magazine . . . er . . . a newspaper that he doesn't like the text. He thinks it's all wrong what they say.*
Teacher   *And what do you think?*
Student 6   *It's a bit . . . er . . . There are some pop groups like [. . .], they are not so aggressive, but in some concerts in London or in New York or so . . . The fans are very aggressive . . .*

7 Text production

While the students had been reading, the teacher had written on the board a number of text lead-ins which seemed likely to encourage transfer of the theme of crowding into everyday experience:

- *My feeling in the crowd was . . .*
- *When I felt the others close to me, . . .*
- *The first word that came to my mind was . . .*
- *The pushing and pressing reminded me of . . .*
- *When I felt the pressure, I wanted to . . .*
- *I often feel pressure. I . . .*

Each student chose one of the text lead-ins and completed it to make a short text thus moving from text reception to text production. Figure 3.5 is an example of one of these texts.

> My feeling in the crowd was good and not so good. The reason why I had a good feeling is that all members where in the circle and nobody was out of it. It gave me the feeling that we are all friends and that there is nobody alone. The other feeling was not good, because I throught for a moment about a . . .

Figure 3.5

8 Text publication

The students' texts were put up in suitable spots around the classroom, set far enough apart for everyone to be able to wander around the room and read them without crowding. This mode of publication seemed particularly appropriate here, as texts so real in emotional content need to be read privately.

It was up to the students how many texts they read and how long they spent reading them (five minutes in the trial class). This was in line with our long-term aim of movement towards independence in learning.

9 Feedback

The teacher then asked the students to give feedback to one or more fellow writers on the language and content of their piece of writing.

Here is an extract from one feedback conversation (about a different piece of writing from that in Fig. 3.5):

Student 1 *You write . . . I felt good and bad . . . but I feel you can't feel good and bad at the same time.*

Student 2 *Yes . . . I know what you mean, but I felt bad because it was hot and I don't feel good when it is hot and I felt good because we were all together.*

Student 1 *(reads in a low voice) I think some people would like to make some-body angry . . . That's good because we were all together . . . Yes, here I have the same feeling, but I think it wasn't hot. I think the place was too small.*

Student 2 *Yes, that's right.*

etc.

CONCLUDING DISCUSSION

When you tell your students exactly what to read (and possibly also exactly when to read it), you are depriving them of the whole natural process of deciding to read something, seeing what there is to read, forming images of what the different choices might contain and, finally, choosing something to read on the basis of these speculative images. It is important – and possible – to compensate for this loss. One purpose of this unit has been to suggest some ways of doing this in class; that is, how to generate and exploit interest in and experience with a text topic before the text is encountered. Another purpose has been to suggest a method of organising critical analysis of a text.

A rationale for this method is that association of vocabulary with clear mental images of situations (including an emotional dimension) is now well known to increase memorability, and so learning. In addition, attention to the emotional dimension of a text increases the quality of any student writing which is based on that text. Regular attention to this dimension raises the quality of student writing generally as it inclines students to write with more of a view to having an effect on a reader. The 'publication' activity also has its long-term pay-off in students writing with heightened awareness of the need to be intelligible and interesting for a specific readership.

Variations

Again, like all our units, this one can be adapted to different levels, age groups and needs, and also different texts. One colleague, who teaches in a quiet rural district, used 'The Crowd in the Noose' activity to prepare her class for a text about a traffic jam in New York, a text which she felt would otherwise strike them as too remote to be of interest.

Here is another activity which, like 'The Crowd in the Noose', has a strong emotional impact that can be exploited to prepare a class you know fairly well for any text about personal change. (We learnt this from Gundl Kutschera, a trainer in Neuro-Linguistic Programming.)

1 Tell everyone that they are (literally) going to go for a half-hour walk with a purpose but no destination.
2 Tell them to ask themselves the following three questions while they are gone:
   • Where am I? (= The present stage of my development).
   • Where am I going? (= What are my aims?)
   • What do I need to learn in order to get there? (= What knowledge and abilities do I need?)

   Make sure that everyone is clear about the significance of each question.
3 Tell them that instead of trying to answer the questions in words, they should stroll around and allow their subconscious to notice or imagine, for each question, an object (e.g. a stone or a leaf) or a natural property (e.g. the warmth of the sun or the colours of the rainbow) which symbolises an answer.
4 Ask your students to bring their objects back to class, if possible. When they return, ask them to form groups of three. In turn, each student reports their findings while the other two, by asking questions or otherwise encouraging the reporter to elaborate, try to learn as much as they can about the reasons for each choice of object or property.

   Of course, every participant must maintain a strictly non-judgmental stance. Students often report gaining deep and surprising insights about themselves and each other.

Housework

Developing a listening comprehension exercise into a real language encounter

LEVEL
Intermediate +

TIME
6–8 hours

TRIAL CLASS
Twenty-eight fourteen- to fifteen-year-olds in their fourth year of English; three fifty-minute lessons a week

AIMS
Making classroom listening activities relevant, interesting and motivating; sensitising students to the sub-skill of active listening; moving from a listening to a role play; guiding students towards the formation of better free communication skills, specifically, the mechanics of turn-taking; encouraging students to talk about their opinions and feelings

Language areas and skills
Oral fluency; listening; writing; reading; discourse features in a text; vocabulary keyed to text and topic

Materials
Stage 1: Hand-out of street map and shopping list (Fig. 4.1, p. 53)
Stage 2: Audio-cassettes from *Task Listening* (Blundell and Stokes 1981)
Stage 5: Display of statements on paper or OHP transparencies (Fig. 4.5, p. 58); hand-out of structures to use in discussion (tables on p. 59); poster of expressions used in turn-taking (optional), (Fig. 4.6, p. 60)
Stage 6: Hand-out of model group report (p. 60)
Stage 10: Hand-outs of grid (Fig. 4.7, p. 62) and 'Chapman Family Contract' (Fig. 4.8, p. 63)

BACKGROUND AND RATIONALE

Nowadays it is easy for teachers to provide varied practice in the listening skill. Both coursebooks and skills books offer a wide range of listening materials for learners of all levels. However, these materials – as potentially interesting in content as they may be – are often remote from the concerns of students, particularly ones learning in a non-English-speaking country. One of our aims here has been to show how students can be brought to see what their reality has in common with that presented in a recording set in a foreign culture.

We will also try to show a way of exploiting a text that is linguistically above the level of your students – a way that enables them to finish the listening encouraged by their success at hearing the most important information, and that also moves on to useful speaking practice.

UNIT SUMMARY

Lesson 1

1 Pre-listening scene setting

Students speculate about hand-out (map and shopping list, see Fig. 4.1).

2 Presentation of the listening text

Students extract key bits of information from a listening text (Blundell and Stokes 1981) and label shops shown on the map.

3 Taking on roles

Role plays (teacher–students; students–teacher; students–students)

Lesson 2

4 Bridging the gap to the students' world

Elicit or present necessary vocabulary. List it on the board. Then rub it out and rewrite it in a structure suggested entirely, or partly, by the students. The students write simple sentences which they expand and build into texts.

5 Content-oriented groupwork

Students discuss some provocative statements presented in speech bubbles. If necessary, hand out sheets which provide useful language structures and/or produce a poster showing language that is useful in facilitating turn-taking in group discussion.

Lesson 3

6 Reporting on the group discussions

Given an imaginary group report as a model text, the groups report the results of their discussions to the whole class.

7 Preparing role plays

Students imagine family situations which feature solutions to some of the problems raised so far. They then prepare role plays based on these imaginary family situations.

8 Role play

Students present their role plays to the class.

Lesson 4

9 Process evaluation

Students discuss the solutions shown in the role plays and discuss their in-role experiences.

10 Text presentation

Present the 'Chapman Family Contract' to show the kinds of solutions that a family might reach. Give out a grid to guide the students in drawing essential information from the text.

Unit 5 *Class contract*, shows how to develop work done in this unit and apply it to personal interaction in the class.

1 Pre-listening scene setting

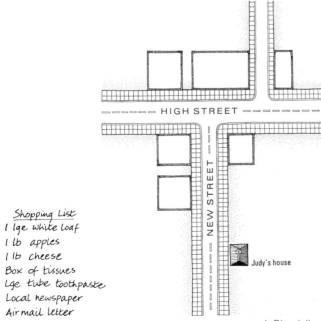

Shopping List
1 lge white loaf
1 lb apples
1 lb cheese
Box of tissues
Lge tube toothpaste
Local newspaper
Air mail letter

Figure 4.1

L Blundell and J Stokes, *Task Listening*, CUP 1981 (1) p. 32

The teacher began by handing out a copy of a map and a shopping list (Fig. 4.1) and encouraging the students to speculate about the use to which they would be put. She accepted their contributions appreciatively, avoiding such stereotypical teacher-like behaviour as the echoing of student contributions (e.g. Teacher: 'What's this?' / Student: 'A map.' / Teacher: 'A map.').

2 Presentation of the listening text

First the teacher asked the class to predict what the listening text was going to be about. When they had made their guesses, she asked the students to label the buildings on the map as they heard clues in the recorded dialogue. Here is the tapescript of the dialogue:

Fiona   *OK Judy, I've got the list here. Erm . . . now, d'you think there's anything else you need?*

Judy   *No, that's everything actually. You don't mind going, Fiona, do you?*

Fiona   *No! I like shopping, and anyway, I'd like to find my way around here a little bit.*

Judy   *Oh, that's tremendous then. Well, shall we just run through the shopping list to make sure you know where all the shops are?*

Fiona   *Good idea. Fine. OK, here goes. Er, the first thing I've got is one large white loaf. Now, where shall I get that from?*

Judy   *Yes, if you get that from the baker's . . . (From the baker's) so that it's nice and fresh.*

Fiona   *Yes, OK, erm . . . how do I get there from here?*

Judy   *Well, it's not very far. You just go down New Street, which is where we are, (Yes) and it's on the other side of the road on the corner of High Street and New Street, so it's on the left.*

Fiona   *Good. Fine. Got that . . . and er . . . a pound of apples. Now, where'd you usually buy your apples?*

Judy   *At the greengrocer's (Uh-huh) you know the one. It's very very close. It's next to the baker's . . . actually before you get to the baker's.*

Fiona   *On the left-hand side of New Street?*

Judy   *Right. It's on the same side of the road as the baker's.*

Fiona   *OK, erm . . . a pound of cheese.*

Judy   *Yes, you get that from the Co-op, where there's plenty of choice.*

Fiona   *From the Co-op. (Yes) Mm-mm.*

Judy   *And again that's quite easy to get to. (Mm) You go right the way down New Street until you get to the High Street.*

Fiona   *Oh, so it's opposite.*

Judy   *That's right, and (Uh-huh) the Co-op is on the other side of the road just opposite New Street and you can't miss it.*

Fiona   *Yes. OK. So, that's er . . . cheese at the Co-op, er . . . box of tissues. Now, where would you like me to get those from?*

Judy   *Probably the chemist is best, (The chemist, mm) I should think. It's usually* cheaper there. (OK) And that's on this side of the road, so you just go down New Street and it's on the right. It's on . . . again on the corner of High Street and New Street, just opposite the baker's.

Fiona Oh yes. Yes, I remember. Yes. Fine. Erm . . . and a large tube of toothpaste. Er . . . shall I get that from the chemist as well?

Judy Probably best to, yes. It'll save you time too.

Fiona OK. Fine. And er . . . oh, the . . . yes, the local newspaper.

Judy Yes, get that from the newsagent's.

Fiona Yes, right.

Judy Now, that is in the High Street (Yes) on the opposite corner to the Co-op. There's a very small street in between.

Fiona Oh, I think I've seen it. (Yes) Yes, it's actually on the corner.

Judy It's on the corner opposite the Co-op – quite a small shop.

Fiona Fine. And last of all airmail letter . . . an airmail letter.

Judy Ah, yes. Now if you get that from the Post Office (Mm-mm) which is next to the Co-op the other side. There's the . . .

Fiona Next to the Co-op . . .

Judy Yes, so it's on High Street (Yes) and it's . . . there's the Post Office, then the Co-op, and then over the road are the newsagent's. So there's those three shops in the High Street.

Fiona Right then. Well, I'll be off now.

Judy That's lovely. Thanks very much.

Fiona OK. See you in half an hour or so.

Judy OK. See you later.

Fiona Bye.

Judy Bye.

L Blundell and J Stokes, *Task Listening*, CUP 1981 (2) p. 76

After the students had listened to the dialogue once, the teacher gave them a minute to compare their labels in pairs. When she asked if everything was clear, some students said they did not agree about their labels so the teacher decided to play the dialogue a second time.

Normally, when we hear someone speaking, we are already in possession of clues which give us a framework for interpreting what we hear. For example, the setting, who they are, what they might want and so on. The copy of the map and the shopping list not only provided some of this framework, but also helped to make the students aware of basic language items in the dialogue which they would need to know about later on (e.g. street names and shopping goods). (The tapescript of the dialogue was never shown to the students.)

The listening activity prepared the students for the role play by giving them a model for each of the two roles. In the following stage the students remembered the models and thus identified with them.

3 Taking on roles

Now that the students were familiar with the gist and key language in the listening text, the role play work began:

Teacher   *We are at Judy's house now. I'll do the shopping for you. So you can send me shopping now. Are you ready?*
Students   *Yes.*
Teacher   *What do you want me to get for you?*
Student 1 *A loaf of bread.*
Teacher   *Where can I get that?*
Student 2 *At the baker's. You must go down the . . .*

At this point oral practice with the dialogue was very controlled – like a drill, in fact. Nevertheless, it was meaningful and communicatively relevant, and began the process of role identification.

Beginning dialogue work in this fashion tends to foster authenticity in intonation, look and gesture. You will probably need to intervene occasionally with corrections, but these should be in a style as close as possible to the style of the dialogue itself. (This is sometimes called 'natural response' correction.)

Teacher *Where do you usually buy your apples?*
Student *At the greengrocer's.*
Teacher *Where's that?*
Student *Before you getting to the baker's.*
Teacher *Ah. Before I get to the baker's. And the toothpaste?*
Student *I always buy toothpaste by the chemist.*
Teacher *At the chemist's, you mean?*
Student *At the chemist's, yes.*

Next, the roles were swapped, with the teacher taking the one that the students had taken before. Then the students practised the dialogue in pairs, all at the same time. In each pair one student used the map as a memory aid in giving directions to the student who had the role of the stranger.

Comment: Some teachers are afraid that in an activity like this students will make masses of mistakes and even, in a sense, be practising error-ridden language. However, you can view an activity like this as an opportunity for you to circulate among the students and listen in, in order to form a clear idea of their difficulties with both the language and the task. This can be invaluable in deciding what you need to reteach in order to help students to overcome their most common, most basic or most easily changeable errors.

4 Bridging the gap to the students' world

The teacher then asked the students whether any of them ever did the shopping or helped with other household chores. This involved the elicitation and presentation of a certain amount of new vocabulary which the teacher wrote on the board. When the necessary vocabulary had been elicited, the teacher cleaned the board and then re-elicited the same vocabulary after asking the students not to look at any notes they had taken. As they recalled the vocabulary, the teacher, with their help, grouped words into small collocations and ordered them as shown below:

Household chores	Equipment
wash the dishes	*dishwasher*
iron the clothes	*vacuum cleaner*
sweep the floor	*stove*
hoover the carpets	*spin-drier*
do the cooking	*iron*
water the flowers	
clean the windows	Adjectives
mend the clothes	*interesting*
mow the lawn	*necessary*
tidy up the rooms	*useful*
make the beds	*useless*
go shopping	*dull*
lay the table	*silly*

Piepho (1982, pp. 11 ff.) suggests a simple procedure whereby students who are given such structured lists of vocabulary can move in a relatively short time to production of meaningful texts. The first step here was, that the teacher asked the students to produce simple sentences, as in Figure 4.2, using words from the list if they wished.

> I must help my mother.
> I don't like housework,
> It's for girls.

Figure 4.2

The students then expanded these simple sentences by adding in words (*sometimes*, *often* and *usually*) provided by the teacher (see Fig. 4.3).

> I sometimes help my brother to bake a
> cake. I never do the cleaning. My mother
> usually makes the bed in my room.

Figure 4.3

Next they added the words *and, but, therefore, that's why* and *for*. This resulted in longer sentences but ones still not too demanding in terms of grammar and text structure (see Fig. 4.4).

> House work is not very interesting. That is why I never help my mother. But on Sundays I usually make the breakfast for the all family, therefore my mother likes Sundays very much. Last Sunday I could not make the breakfast, because I was ill in bed. I had a flu.

Figure 4.4

By putting their thoughts down on paper, the learners rehearsed language they would need in discussion later on.

5 Content-oriented groupwork

Next the teacher displayed statements which were related to familiar aspects of students' lives. These statements were written on large sheets of paper in the form of speech bubbles (see Fig. 4.5).

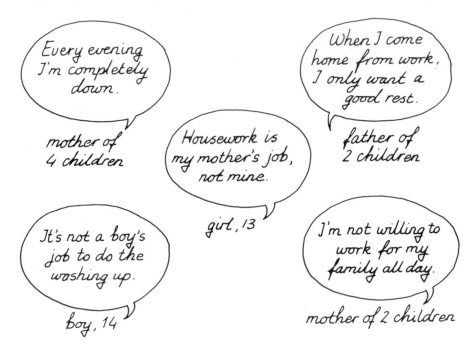

Figure 4.5

The teacher organised the students into groups of five or six, saying that in a couple of minutes they should discuss the statements in the speech bubbles. In order to prevent group discussion from floundering or drifting into the mother tongue, the teacher gave each student a hand-out showing the language most useful for the discussion. The discussion phrases were presented in the form of substitution tables:

What the	boy girl mother	said is	also not sometimes	a problem for	me. my mother. my family. ....

I think it's	a pity unfair not right OK	that the	mother boy girl	has to do all work. does not help. need not wash up. does not go shopping. wants to ....

I ——— Do you	always never usually sometimes hardly ever	help with . . . do the . . . go . . .	. ?

Naturally, it is impossible to completely predict what students are going to want to say in such discussions. We tried, however, to make our hand-outs as useful as possible by composing them to reflect the class's interests and language level.

The teacher made sure that everyone understood all this language, gave them time to select what they wanted to say and then asked the groups to begin their discussions.

Teenage learners need encouragement in turn-taking if some are not to dominate and others to be left out of group discussions. A display such as the one shown in Figure 4.6 can figure in regular training in turn-taking.

Here is an excerpt from the lesson transcript:

Student 1 *I always help my mother in the kitchen.*
Student 2 *I think it's not OK that the mother does the housework alone. I always . . . not always, but sometimes help my mother. What do you think, S?*
Student 3 *Yes. I do, too. But I don't like to wash up.*
Student 4 *I think it's not fair when the father come home from work he only want to have a rest. I think he can help the mother and the children with the housework.*
Student 2 *And you, A?*
Student 5 *I clean the shoes for all my mother and my father.*
Student 3 *That's not right.*

Teacher *Why do you think that's not right?*
Student 3 *The father make it dirty . . .*
Student 4 *(to Student 5) You don't do it. I think that's not right.*
Student 5 *Yes.*
Student 3 *I think that's silly.*

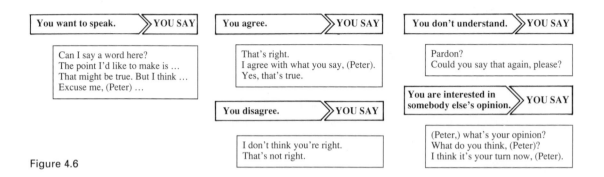

Figure 4.6

6 Reporting on the group discussions

After the discussions in groups, the teacher asked the students to write reports on the *process* as well as the results of their discussions. She laid the groundwork for this by giving out a model group report. This served two main purposes. It showed how to summarise the content of a discussion and it also indicated important elements of discussion as a process. That is, besides being a model for language, length and format, it figured in a campaign to make students aware of the pre-conditions and dynamics of successful communication.

Here is an example of a report created by one of the groups in the trial class:

For us the discussion was very interesting. We don't think that everything that people said about housework is right. We all understand what the two mothers said, but some of us also do not help our mothers at all. We had no problems with our English in the discussion, but sometimes it was difficult to understand each other.

7 Preparing role plays

The students read out their group reports to the whole class. Afterwards the teacher summarised the main points of conflict and then put the students into groups again and asked them to imagine family situations in which solutions to the conflicts would be possible. The teacher also asked each group to prepare a role play based on these situations. She reminded them they would need to decide the roles and the setting and also develop a rough plot.

Once the students decided these things, they practised their role plays in their groups. (See the discussion of how a role play can be built up in Unit 1, Stages 9 and 10.)

8 Role play

Here is an excerpt from one role play:

Student 1 *I'm the grandmother.*
Student 2 *I'm Angela.*
Student 3 *I'm Peter.*
Student 4 *I'm Eve.*
Student 5 *And I'm the mother.*
Student 3 *Someone must go out with the dog.*
Student 4 *I don't like to go out with the dog. This is grandmother's work.*
Student 1 *This is your work.*
Student 4 *Oh no! Angela, you must go out with the dog.*
Student 2 *I must make the beds.*
Student 3 *I like to make the beds.*
Student 5 *(enters) What's the matter? Stop that noise.*
Student 4 *Er . . . she don't . . . he don't like to wash the car.*
Student 5 *You must wash the car. You must clean the windows. You must go out with the dog and you must make the beds.*
Student 2 *I must wash the windows? We have ten windows in the house!*
Student 3 *Wash the car? I? (annoyed)*
Student 4 *I don't want to make the beds.*
Student 1 *(sighing) OK. I go out with the dog.*

9 Process evaluation

In the meta-discussion that followed, the teacher and class talked about what it was like for students to play people in situations different from their own. Then teacher and students decided whether and how the role plays suggested workable solutions to the problems that had come up earlier in the group discussions in Stage 5.

As it happens, the role plays do not usually include real solutions to the problems they are built around. These are typically repressed or falsely solved by means of traditional avoidance strategies. For example, in the excerpt above, nobody actually said they were willing to do the housework. Instead of looking for a fair solution and dealing frankly with matters of conflict, the grandmother offers a pseudo-solution by volunteering to do the chores, which, of course, makes it unnecessary for any of the other members of the family to change their behaviour. You can work to change the attitudes that underlie these pseudo-solutions by eliciting the consequences of the different behaviours involved and by guiding your class in a consideration of the attitudes and behaviours in terms of fairness v. tradition. (It may be necessary to discuss these questions in the students' mother tongue, if their command of the target language is still weak.) The insights students gain from these discussions have the long-term potential to transfer to the classroom and result in more considerate and cooperative interaction.

10 Text presentation

In order to indicate a possible alternative solution to a problematic family situation, the teacher handed out a grid to complete (Fig. 4.7) and then the 'Chapman Family Contract' (Fig. 4.8). The assumption was that the reading would be easier for the students because the issues it raised had been thoroughly contextualised in the preceding stages of the unit.

Name of person	is allowed to	is not allowed to	has to	should

I think I don't think	it's	good fair wise	....

Figure 4.7

The students' task was to enter the key elements of the charter into the grid. As well as focusing the students' attention on the main topics of the charter, the grid provided them with key expressions which they could use in the subsequent group discussion (e.g.: 'I think it is fair that the children in the family are allowed to stay up as long as they want to.'). The grid also helped students to break up this syntactically complex text into simpler units and later provided them with a framework for writing of their own (as in the following unit).

After reading and filling out their grids, the students discussed the charter in groups. This brought together all the threads of the unit so far: the students' own experiences, the solutions and suggestions given in the charter and their experiences in the role play and the meta-discussion stages.

```
                        CONTRACT
                 for the Chapman Family

HOUSEWORK:              All members of the family - young and old - must do their
                        fair share of housework.
                        A list of things to do will be hung up each week.

FREE TIME:              Children and parents have an equal right to free time!

VISITORS:               Children have a right to bring friends home whenever they
                        like.

BEDTIME:                Bedtime shall be fixed according to age. Over 15s may go
                        to bed when they like.

RULES FOR PARENTS:      • Parents must not break promises.
                        • They must not suddenly change what has been fixed.
                        • They must not criticise their children in public.

NOTE:   Parents are not always right.

                 Signed:
                     John Chapman (Father, teacher)
                       Mary Chapman (Mother, social worker)
                     Susan Chapman (aged 16, at comprehensive school)
                     Andrew Chapman (aged 14,  "    "               ")
```

Figure 4.8

CONCLUDING DISCUSSION

The main threads of the sequence of activities described above are as follows:

Firstly, we have tried to show how stimulation of students' affective interest in a topic can have pay-offs in productive work (here, preparation for and performance of role plays) after a listening activity.

Secondly, we have shown how in our trial class a listening grid was used for the dual purpose of (a) encouraging students to listen for the key messages in a listening text and discouraging them from overstretching themselves by trying to hear the exact wording throughout, and (b) providing a framework for structuring and prompting follow-on role plays.

Another strand in this unit has been the importance of active listening, that is listening with identification, with a view to eventual participation. By identifying with the roles of the speakers in the recorded listening (Stage 3) and drawing on their own experiences at home (Stage 4), the students gradually became able, and willing, to express their own opinions and feelings. Especially in Stages 8 and 9 (conflict resolution), it was important for students to *listen with involvement*. Pike and Selby (1988, p. 125) put it this way: 'Listening requires a combination of hearing what another person says and active involvement in what she is saying.' They cast interesting light on this notion of active, or empathic, listening through an analysis of the meaningful components of the Chinese character for *listen* (Figure 4.9).

Figure 4.9

G Pike and P Selby, *Global Teacher, Global Learner*, Hodder & Stoughton 1988 p. 125

A similar perspective on listening is evident in the following extract from 'Momo', a story by Michael Ende. Both the Chinese character and the story can stimulate fruitful classroom meta-discussions on listening.

Momo could listen in such a way that worried and indecisive people knew their own minds from one moment to the next, or shy people felt suddenly confident and at ease, or downhearted people felt happy and hopeful. And if someone felt that his life had been an utter failure, and that he himself was only one among millions of wholly unimportant people who could be replaced as easily as broken windowpanes, he would go and pour out his heart to Momo. And, even as he spoke, he would come to realize by some mysterious means that he was absolutely wrong: that there was only one person like himself in the whole world, and that, consequently, he mattered to the world in his own particular way. Such was Momo's talent for listening.

Michael Ende, *Momo*, Penguin 1984 pp. 18–19

Class contract

A class and their teacher decide on their own ground rules

LEVEL
Lower – mid-intermediate

TIME
5–8 hours

TRIAL CLASS
Twenty-two twelve- to thirteen-year-olds in their third year of English; three fifty-minute lessons a week

AIMS
Bulding up the mutual trust required for discussion of feelings normally concealed from teachers; developing empathy; encouraging reflection on classroom roles and behaviours; sensitising students to basic factors in conflict resolution

Language areas and skills
Oral fluency; expressions of agreement and disagreement

Materials
Stage 1:   Collage of do's and don'ts (this can be in L1)
Stage 2:   Paper for students to draw signs on
Stage 3:   Blu-tack
Stage 4:   Substitution table (Fig. 5.3, p. 70); large blank paper speech bubbles; felt-tip pens
Stage 5:   Blu-tack
Stage 9:   Two large sheets of paper for the class contract

BACKGROUND AND RATIONALE

It might at first appear artificial to have students use the foreign language to discuss such things as how they feel about their classes and it might, as well, appear demotivating for students to use the foreign language to express such things as their irritation or anger about homework, their worries about grades and so forth.

We have, however, noticed in our work with students that despite their difficulties with the foreign language and with presumably unfamiliar discourse customs, they have often participated in discussions in the foreign language with great interest: the primary concern was always meaning and content, not the language itself.

C Black and W Butzkamm, *Klassengespräche-Kommunikativer Unterricht: Beispiel und Anregung*, Quelle und Meyer 1977 p. 109

Our experience strongly suggests that Black and Butzkamm are right. Once English has been established as the main medium of communication during the English lesson, it is quite possible to take the here and now of the classroom as a source for talking points, not just from time to time, but as a matter of course. In fact, we have frequently seen that students, both adults and adolescents, often find that there are some topics it is easier to discuss in English than in their mother tongue. For example, in talking about feelings, students may find that using the foreign language enables them to express thoughts which, if the mother tongue were used, would go against certain taboos. Use of the foreign language seems to give some students the feeling that the discussion is taking place beyond the reach of these taboos.

In planning this unit we wanted to test our assumption that, by building up trust in the classroom, we may be able to create a climate that encourages students to express the feelings that they have in these taboo areas. We decided to begin by making students aware of the constraints on them in everyday life and then move to a discussion of interaction in the classroom and the constraints involved there. Finally, by getting students to reflect on their roles and behaviour, we hoped to lead some to modify their classroom behaviour for the better.

Additionally, as in the previous unit, a deeper aim was to help students:
- learn to deal with conflict openly by understanding the feelings, attitudes and behaviour of others
- develop the habit of considering if or how to modify their own behaviour in order to lessen conflict.

UNIT SUMMARY
Lesson 1

1 Brainstorming
Confront the students with signs bearing do's and don'ts. They respond spontaneously.

2 Drawing
Students draw additional signs on sheets of paper.

3 Focusing on the topic
In a quiet period students ponder the messages in these signs.

4 Defining norms
Students write do's and don'ts on prepared speech bubbles.

Lesson 2

5 Counter-arguments
In pairs or groups, students select one speech bubble and use it as the beginning of a role play dialogue. Students write down their dialogues.

6 Conflict dialogue
The students present their role plays to the whole class.

Lesson 3

7 Widening the topic
Present the 'Chapman Family Contract' as an example of possible solutions in one conflict area (see Fig. 4.8, p. 63).

8 Content-oriented groupwork
The prompts from the grid help in eliciting suggestions for a 'class contract'. Initially, students note down points individually, then in groups as a basis for further work.

Lessons 4 and 5

9 Class parliament
In a whole group session students discuss and select the suggestions and then incorporate them into a final copy of a class contract which everyone signs. It is put on the wall for permanent display.

1 Brainstorming

The teacher presented, or rather confronted, the class with a collage of everyday signs that say what to do and what not to do. The example in Figure 5.1 comes from a magazine article about the proliferation of signs that children are faced with daily.

Figure 5.1

From *Unser Kind*, 4, 1979 p. 71

At first the teacher was silent and waited for students to comment spontaneously. When comment began to flag, he quickly put these prompts on the board:

I think it's unfair that . . .
I can't understand why . . .
I think children should be allowed to . . .
Grown-ups often . . .

He waited patiently and gave students lots of time to think and speak.

2 Drawing

When comment showed signs of drying up, the teacher passed out large sheets of paper and asked students to draw other signs that they saw in their daily lives, both inside and outside school. He stressed that what he had in mind was not carefully drawn works of sign-painter's art.

One by one, the students presented their drawings to the class. Each time, the 'audience' speculated about why the speaker had drawn that particular sign. The speaker either said 'Yes, that's what I meant' or explained what it was that they actually did mean.

Rationale: The aim in asking for more constraining and prohibitory signs was not to invite students to rebel against every constraint on their behaviour, but to begin to make them aware that constraints can be more or less sensible and to set the stage for later discussion of how some could be modified.

3 Focusing on the topic

After all the students had presented their signs, they stuck them on the wall. The teacher then asked them to ponder the signs for a while and to try to think of other constraints and prohibitions affecting them in their daily lives. After soliciting, and briefly discussing their contributions, the teacher then focused the discussion on their lives in school. He began by asking for complete silence, stressing that silence was *essential* for what they were about to do.

He then asked them to close their eyes and think back to and briefly relive in-school experiences of constraints and prohibitions.

Comment: It can be a little difficult to manage a successful reflection time with a class that has never tried this kind of thing before. Younger students especially can have difficulty at first in settling down to this kind of activity. They will probably be unused to taking their own feelings and attitudes seriously (much less discussing them, even in their mother tongue), and so may find it quite difficult to be quiet in the beginning. They may giggle, be uncooperative or even disruptive.

In such a case it can be a good idea either later or right then and there to bring the students' feelings out into the open. Take care to be non-judgmental and to clearly show your class that you take their comments seriously. Such whole class discussions can end in understandings which you and the students can refer back to later. One way of doing this is to write a symbol or word on the board and tell students to remember the discussion they just had whenever they see it written on the board. The result can be much more desirable than that you could achieve by intervening verbally. One symbol we have used is shown in Figure 5.2.

Figure 5.2

4 Defining norms

In this stage the students reported the experiences they had recalled during the reflective phase. For this they used basic language presented in a substitution table on a poster (see Fig. 5.3). Though he did help with language, the teacher added no evaluative feedback.

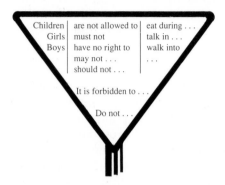

Figure 5.3

The teacher then handed out large blank speech bubbles made of paper and asked the students to fill them in, in English, with do's and don'ts. He stressed that the sentences should be written in large letters so they could be read from a distance. Here are the (corrected) statements that the students wrote:

It is forbidden to walk on the grass.
Children are not allowed to smoke in school.
Children are not allowed to shout at their parents.
Children must not wear shoes in the classroom.
Children must not talk during the lesson.
Boys have no right to say girls are silly.
Children are often not allowed to chew gum.
Children have no right to tell their parents that they should not speak at dinner.
Children are not allowed to say what they want at school.
Children are not allowed to go out after nine o'clock.
Children are not allowed to talk during most lessons.
Normally, children are not allowed to do the same things as grown-ups.

5 Counter-arguments

Next, the teacher and students stuck the speech bubbles up on the walls around the class. The teacher then put the students into pairs (groups of four also work). Each pair selected one or more speech bubbles which had an emotional impact on one or both of them. Then they used what was written in (one of) their speech bubble(s) as the beginning of a dialogue which they then worked out and wrote down. When these were finished and had been rehearsed to the point where both partners agreed how it went, they wrote it down turn-by-turn on other speech bubble cut-outs as shown in Figure 5.4.

Figure 5.4

The next step was further rehearsal (in pairs) of the finished dialogues in the speech bubbles.

Comment: With a class that has never done this kind of work before, it helps if you and the class compose one speech bubble dialogue together before pairs or groups write their own. One way of doing this is to stand at the board eliciting ideas for filling in one blank speech bubble. When everyone agrees on what to put in the bubble, you or a 'secretary' can fill it in and stick it on the board. You then move to the next bubble.

6 Conflict dialogue

The pairs now acted out the dialogues in front of the whole class.

7 Widening the topic

In our experience, such role plays hardly ever feature such an amicable ending as in Figure 5.4. What comes to light is very often a reflection of the conflicts students have in their everyday lives but which they do not really know how to resolve. Accordingly, in the trial class, the teacher followed on from the role play stage by summarising the difficulties involved in solving conflict. He then guided the discussion on to other conflict areas such as the family, games and sports. The teacher and class discussed possible solutions to some of these conflicts. As often happens, students made the point that people can avoid conflict if they follow certain rules.

As the class had already done the unit on 'Housework', the teacher was able to refer back to the 'Chapman Family Contract' (Fig. 4.8, p. 63), whose function of establishing rules by group consent the students were now better equipped to appreciate. If a similar unit has not been done, hand out this contract along with the accompanying grid (Fig. 4.7, p. 62). The class can, at this point, work on the contract following the procedure outlined in Stage 10 of Unit 4.

In our class, students and teacher discussed the possibility of composing something similar to the 'Chapman Family Contract' for guiding personal interaction in class.

8 Content-oriented groupwork

The teacher asked the students to work individually at first, and note down any ideas they had for points that should be included in a class contract. Then he asked the students to work in groups and list the problems they encountered in personal interaction in the class. He stressed that the aim was to find *realistic* solutions to these problems and that this would demand some willingness to compromise. The search for solutions began with a 'secretary' in each group jotting down members' contributions under these headings which the teacher had written on the board:

Problems in our class   *Things we do not like*   *Rules we'd like to have*

Groupwork like this moves along faster if the secretary records contributions in keyword form. To exemplify this, the teacher gave the following explanation.

I, for example, am not too happy about the fact that it always takes such a long time at the beginning of each lesson to collect all the homework books. (Teacher goes to board and notes down 'Classroom organisation' in the problem column and 'Collecting homework takes too much time' under the 'Things we do not like' heading.) So a rule I'd like to suggest would be that everybody puts their homework book on my desk during the break before the lesson actually starts. (Teacher writes 'Homework on desk before lesson' in the third column.)

After suggesting this procedure, the teacher also told the group that they would have time towards the end of the activity to work together to produce a summary of their thoughts in sentence form.

Figure 5.5 is an excerpt from the ideas written down by one group. Note that the language that students needed for this had already been worked with, particularly in the activities based on the 'Chapman Family Contract'.

> We would like to chew Chewing-gum. We have to speak english. The students have no right to tell us off. Students have to speak English too. The students should hear to th teacher.

Figure 5.5

9 Class parliament

A spokesperson from each group read their conclusions out to the whole class. With the teacher as facilitator (a student can sometimes assume this role), the whole class discussed the conclusions presented by the various groups.

Language which students might need in order to participate effectively in such a group discussion might be:

I think / In my opinion	it would be	good / useless / silly / fair / unfair	to . . .

I don't agree with what you said about . . .
I don't think it's a good idea to . . .
The thing is, if . . .

Why	don't / can't / shouldn't	we . . . ?	We	can . . . / do . . . / should . . .

The teacher then recorded on a large sheet of paper whatever the whole class had agreed should be in the class contract. A class secretary rewrote this preliminary draft as neatly as possible on another large sheet of paper. Everyone, the teacher included, then signed the contract (see Fig. 5.6), which was thereafter kept on prominent display.

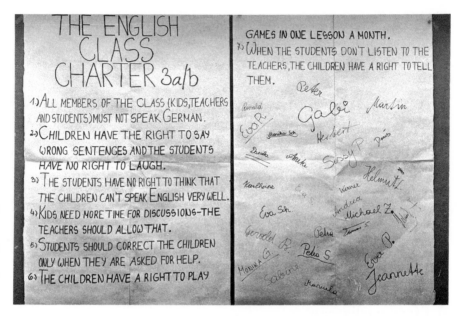

Figure 5.6
The class contract drawn up by the trial class. (The class was regularly observed by trainee teachers whom the children refer to as 'students' in the contract)

CONCLUDING DISCUSSION

The students involved in this trial unit learned that the organisation of their class was not determined solely by the school. They learned that they could discuss and decide on important details. They also learned that they could do this in English.

In general, once students begin to see that the nature and quality of classroom interaction is, in important respects, theirs to decide, discussion of classroom rules and whether and how they should be regulated can become a regular feature. Our experience is that a prerequisite for this stage is a climate of trust. In this unit, we have tried to describe the implementation of several means of working towards realisation of such a climate – that is, creation of silence for students to think in, directed meditation, reflection on past experiences, non-judgmental listening and frankness about one's own position and responsibilities.

As for the contract, it is important to stick to it, otherwise nothing has been gained.

Feelings

Developing awareness about emotions and empathy with others

LEVEL
Lower intermediate

TIME
3–4 hours

TRIAL CLASS
Thirty fourteen-year-olds in their third year of English; three fifty-minute lessons a week

AIMS
Establishing links between students' feelings about the world and the reality of the language class; preparing students to talk about feelings in English; developing students' and your own ability to take classmates'/students' feelings seriously

Language areas and skills
Oral fluency; listening; writing; functions and vocabulary for the expression/description of feelings

Materials
Stage 1: Pictures of people expressing different emotions; Blu-tack
Stage 2: Hand-out of substitution table (p. 78)
Stage 3: Hand-out of diagram (Fig. 6.3, p. 80)
Stage 5: Recorded listening text and hand-out of grid (Fig. 6.4, p. 81)
Stage 6: Hand-out of diagram (Fig. 6.5, p. 82)

BACKGROUND AND RATIONALE

Like all the other activity sequences described in this book, this one was designed to encourage students to reveal something of their real thoughts and concerns in the foreign language classroom.

More specifically, we wanted to show how to establish a link between the students' own feelings about the world and the reality of the language class. Although mainstream language teaching methodology has come around to the view that the feelings of individual students are important and must be taken into consideration, it still seems that one's personality as a student is rarely congruent with one's personality outside class.

UNIT SUMMARY
Lesson 1

1 Brainstorming
Present some magazine pictures or photographs of people expressing different emotions.

2 Speculating about reasons for feelings
Groups discuss one picture and try to agree on the feelings of the person or people shown in the pictures and the reasons why they have these feelings.

Lesson 2

3 Towards the learners' own feelings
Present a list of situations likely to have emotional impact and words for feelings. The students select some of the situations and note down some of the feelings they associate with them.

4 Analysis of feelings
In pairs or groups students compare and discuss their work from Stage 3.

Lesson 3

5 Presentation of listening text
Students listen to a text. A grid is used to guide the students towards an understanding of the feelings implicit in this text.

6 Thinking back/Reflection
The words for feelings that the students have written in the grid are transferred to students' own experiences.

7 Reporting

The students report on the insights they gained in Stage 6.

Lesson 4

8 Dialogue building

Working in pairs, students select one of the original magazine pictures. They write a dialogue between the person or one of the people in the picture and some other person. The dialogue is written inside speech bubbles.

9 Role play

Students act the role plays out in front of the whole class.

1 Brainstorming

The teacher had brought a selection of photos and magazine pictures of people in the grip of powerful emotions. She began by fixing them to the board. Among the photographs were ones stemming from recent well-known events, such as wars and other catastrophes, as well as sporting events and a royal wedding.

To make it easier for the students to interpret the visuals, the teacher first gave them a couple of minutes just to look at the pictures. She then posed questions like the following:

- What has happened to her/him/them?
- What's her/his/their problem?
- What about her/him/them?
- What has happened?
- Do you know why . . . ?

Comment: If your students are used to preparing materials at home for their English classes, you can ask them to collect and organise the display of visuals themselves. One advantage is that the students are better prepared for and more in the mood for what you have planned for them. They learn too that you take them seriously enough to use materials they have made or gathered. We suggest, though, that you do not shift all the work of visuals collection onto the students since the process of finding and choosing visuals often suggests new ways of using them.

The more current the event that a photograph relates, the clearer students' interpretations of these photographs tend to be. On the other hand, if there are some pictures which they are not able to connect with any particular happening students are more able to exercise their imaginations. And this in turn tends to lead to the kind of divergence of opinion that stimulates discussion.

2 Speculating about reasons for feelings

In plenary, the students discussed what they thought the reasons were for the feelings on people's faces. This began to bring students' own memories and associations out into the open. In order to feed in useful language the teacher asked students to refer to a substitution table (presentable on the board or a hand-out):

I think	she he	is	happy sad laughing crying angry afraid of . . .	because	she he	has problems with her mum. likes this beautiful day. has got a new coat. has heard a good joke. has won a bicycle. has lost all her/his pocket money. has no pet. has got a bad mark.

After this, the class moved on to a plenary discussion of one of the photographs in detail. As the discussion developed, the teacher briefly summarised students' comments on the board next to the photo. The students then continued the discussion in groups by speculating about how the people in the other photos felt and what might be running through their minds. Each group discussed one picture, and when they had finished their discussion, the group secretary went to the board and wrote a summary of their discussion next to their picture.

The following sums up one group's interpretation of a photograph of a rather sorrowful-looking boy:

- *he is alone*
- *his girlfriend doesn't love him*
- *has problems – has nobody to talk to*
- *problems at school/with parents*
- *no contact with other people*
- *has problems talking about his feelings*
- *has no work*

As a follow-up activity and a conclusion to this stage, the teacher asked the students to write a short text about a new photograph, which they had to select themselves.

3 Towards the learners' own feelings

The aim of this stage was to guide the students in a shift of focus from the feelings of other people to situations of emotional impact that the students themselves might have experienced. The teacher began this work by noting (on the board) situations and feelings which she thought her students might have experienced (Figs. 6.1 and 6.2).

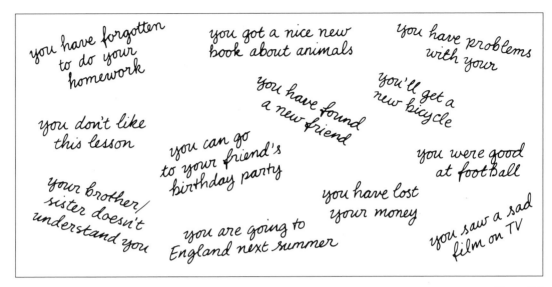

Figure 6.1

Figure 6.2

In order to equip students with more of the words that they might need to discuss their feelings the teacher asked them to close their eyes and think of themselves in one of these situations. After a minute or so of reflection, the teacher asked them to put their feelings into words (German or English). She noted these on the board in English and quickly defined them for those who didn't know them.

Next she gave each student a diagram (Fig. 6.3). The students wrote one of the situations the teacher had presented along each of six rays, as in the diagram. After taking some time to reflect, the students wrote an adjective in the circle at the end of each ray to describe the feelings they would have if they were in that situation.

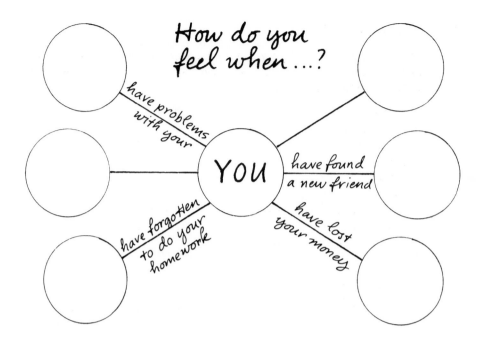

Figure 6.3

4 Analysis of feelings

The aims of this stage were (1) to help develop in the students the habit of talking about their feelings in the foreign language, and (2) to help them to find out about each other's feelings and attitudes so as to foster the mutual understanding essential for social learning.

In groups, the students compared the feelings that they thought they would have in the different situations. As we had hoped, this triggered active discussion not only about what they had written down, but also about situations they actually found themselves in in their everyday lives.

Here is a transcript from one of the group discussions:

Student 1 *How do you feel when you have problems with your parents?*
Student 2 *I feel scared.*
Student 1 *Why?*
Student 2 *Because they are angry.*
Student 1 *What do you do then?*
Student 2 *I go to my room.*
Student 1 *Why?*
Student 2 *I want to play my records.*
Student 1 *Do you feel good then?*
Student 2 *Yes.*
Student 1 *And your parents?*
Student 2 *I like them. Do you like your parents?*
Student 1 *Yes.*

5 Presentation of listening text

In this stage, the teacher's aim was to present a typical textbook dialogue in a way that would help the students to understand the probable emotions of the characters in the dialogues.

Example listening text

Guest *What's that building over there?*
.... *It's a tractor factory. They also make all kinds of machinery.*
Guest *And that building over there?*
.... *That's another factory. Radios, TVs and so on.*
Guest *Is that a factory, too?*
.... *That was a factory. They made clothes. But they closed down.*
Guest *Interesting. My mother and my father work in a clothes factory.*
.... *My father worked in a car factory.*
Guest *Worked?*
.... *At the moment he is out of work.*
Guest *That's very bad.*

H-E Piepho and L Bredella (eds), *Contacts – Integriertes Englischlehrwerk für die Klassen 5–10,*
Kamp 1978 p. 80

This dialogue figures in the textbook as a means of introducing the past simple. It is followed by exercises designed to give students controlled practice with these verb forms. But there is a danger that students will see any text used mainly or merely as vehicle for presenting certain linguistic forms as emotionally empty, for when a teacher uses a text in this fashion the feelings expressed in it will almost certainly be left untapped. Take for example the expression of sympathy in the last line of the dialogue above. One person's father is out of work. But few teachers will even scratch the verbal surface to get at the emotional source.

In order to make the students aware of the emotional implications in the dialogue, the teacher handed out a grid referring to relevant sections in the text. (Fig. 6.4 shows such a grid filled out by one of the students in the trial class.) First, the teacher set students the task of filling in the grid. This they could either do during the listening or from memory afterwards. Finally, using their notes in the grids, the students reported their interpretations to the whole class. This led to a discussion of different perceptions and interpretations.

Figure 6.4

	PERSON	FEELING	REASON
1st person	guest	surprised	parents' jobs
2nd person	German boy	excited / proud	showing guest around
3rd person	father	unsure / worried	out of work

6 Thinking back/Reflection

Next, the students took the vocabulary of emotions from their completed grids and rewrote them into the outer circles of the diagram shown in Figure 6.5. They then wrote the word 'I' in the centre circle. When they had done this, the teacher asked them to think of situations in which they felt the emotions in the outer circles. Each student wrote a brief description of each of these situations on the appropriate ray, for example 'When my hamster died'.

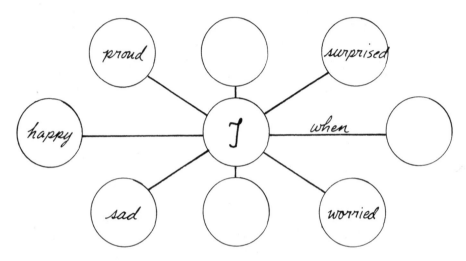

Figure 6.5

7 Reporting

Working in large groups, and using the substitution table below (it was on the board), the students reported on the results of Stage 6.

| I | feel
felt | sad
happy | when . . .
because . . . |
| I'd | feel
not feel | . . .
. . . | if . . . |

8 Dialogue building

The students, working in pairs, selected one of the pictures used in Stage 1 and wrote a dialogue between one or more of the people shown in the picture and some other person not in the picture.

In the trial class the teacher emphasised that the students' behaviour in the role plays should be appropriate for the roles they were playing. In particular, she tried to encourage the students to match their non-verbal behaviour to their verbal performance. She asked the learners to close their eyes and visualise 'their' dialogue in action as vividly as possible. She also asked them to imagine *how* the person they were going to play would behave, especially their gestures, facial expressions, body movements, and tone and loudness of voice. Immediately before the role plays the teacher reminded the students once more of their visualisations and asked them to imagine that they were actually 'slipping into' the person they had imagined in their mind's eye. The teacher allowed for some time before each role play for the students to identify with this inner model and asked them to tell her when they were ready to act out the scene (another small step in encouraging students to take responsibility for the management of learning).

The preparatory work done throughout the unit up to now ensured that the content of the dialogues generally related to the emotional impact of the situation in the picture. Figure 6.6 shows one of the dialogues.

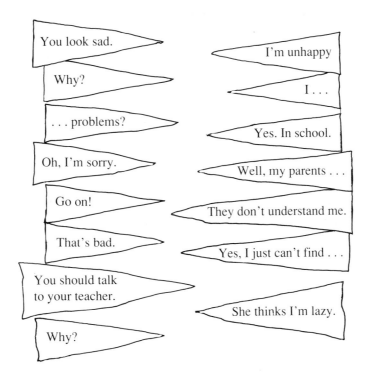

Figure 6.6

9 Role play

Next, the students acted their dialogues out in front of the whole class.

CONCLUDING DISCUSSION

Some teachers report that their students are reluctant to make the personal commitment necessary for such activities to work. Our experience has been that the aloof and sceptical behaviour of these students often stems from a desire not to be taken in by teachers, the direct representatives of an institution they dislike. Additionally, many more students now than previously have been affected by the moral and emotional dislocation resulting from the disintegration of traditional values and communities. All that can be done is to accept these attitudes and respect these students' need for distance. Fortunately, there is almost always a strong underlying desire in these students to get their feelings out into the open. And, as it happens, your class may actually turn out to be the only forum some of your students will have.

However, it is essential that anyone applying a humanistic methodology appreciates how an institutional setting threatens some students. Don't approach a refusal to cooperate naively. Accept it for what it is, not, for example, as motiveless behaviour or a protest against you as a person. If you don't treat it as genuine, students are most unlikely to make the next steps. Very often these are towards respect for what you are trying to achieve and, finally, to agreement with it.

Poetry alive

Stimulating interaction, creativity and depth

LEVEL

Lower intermediate +

TIME

2–3 hours

TRIAL CLASS

Twenty-eight fourteen- to fifteen-year-olds in their fourth year of English; three fifty-minute lessons a week

AIMS

Sensitising students to the expressive power of poetry; stimulating creativity through attention to atmosphere; engaging students in frank but appropriate expression of appreciation and criticism, not only of student writing but also of the unit itself

Language areas and skills

Oral expressions; writing; polite expression of opinion

Materials

Stage 1:   Poems by English-speaking children displayed on board
Stage 2:   Recorded meditative music; symbolic pictures drawn on large sheets of paper
Stage 3:   Cards, scissors, felt-tip pens, magazines, glue, Blu-tack
Stage 4:   Envelopes (one for each student)

BACKGROUND AND RATIONALE

Any poetry that students encounter in the classroom, is usually the work of famous writers. There are obvious difficulties in using literature of this sort in lower-level classes. For one thing, the language is very likely to be too complex; for another, it may be difficult to bring students to see the relevance of the content to their own world of experience.

In this unit we demonstrate a different approach to working with poetry, one which exploits the ability of young people to merge thought and emotion to produce language of special clarity, frankness and expressive power. Additionally, in looking through the poems written by the students in the trial class, we find them convincing evidence that poetry is uniquely suited to the expression of personal identity, a matter of particular concern to adolescents. We have also found that having students write poetry in class is an excellent way of increasing their willingness to be spontaneous and creative on other, more common situations of language production.

The particular questions that shaped our aims in this unit were as follows:

- Is it possible for *in-class* student writing to be as emotionally expressive as that which students can produce in their daily lives outside class – things like diaries, short stories and letters?
- Schools allot considerable time to formal writing. Can some of this time be filled with real literary creativity?
- Can we bridge the gap between students' own worlds of experience and the concerns of school life through poetry?
- Is it really possible for students to write poetry in a foreign language?
- We mentioned earlier that students are sometimes more able to discuss matters in depth and without inhibition in the foreign language. Does this apply to poetry?

We decided to find the answers. We resolved, though, to scrupulously avoid overt correction of errors as teenagers are very quick to notice whether, despite lofty words about creative expression, a teacher's main concern is still with linguistic accuracy.

UNIT SUMMARY
Preparation

1 Sensitisation to poetry
Students read display of poems written by English-speaking children.

Lesson 1

2 Creating the mood
Play soft meditative music as you put half a dozen generative posters up on the wall.

3 Creating posters and poems

Students split into groups and begin working on their posters. After a period of reflection on the posters, the students write poems suggested not only by the poster but also by the process of creating it. Students then sign their poems.

4 Ending the lesson / Concealing the poems

Each student puts their poem in an envelope which is sealed, collected and stored.

Lesson 2

5 Reading others' poems

Start the next lesson with the same music as before. Hand the sealed envelopes out to the class at random. The students open the envelopes and read the poems within.

6 Emotional feedback

Each student writes a letter to the author of the poem they have read.

Lesson 3

Put the poems and perhaps also the feedback letters on the poetry board.

7 Evaluation

You and the students evaluate the unit. Students write feedback texts on the unit and read them out to the whole class.

1 Sensitisation to poetry

In beginning this sequence we tried to make it plain to the students that the term 'poem' is not restricted to highly polished works of art but that poetry comes in a great variety of forms and can be about all kinds of things.

Our way of reinforcing and developing this message was to present poems written by English-speaking children. We arranged a selection of poems from magazines and books on a display board (see p. 93 for some suggested sources of similar poems).

2 Creating the mood

Here are the teacher's recollections of how the first lesson began:

It was the break period between two lessons. There was a lingering tension from the previous maths lesson. The maths teacher was still sitting at her desk hastily correcting a few remaining assignments. The form (homeroom) teacher pressed his way through the turbulence in order to make an announcement. The school bell suddenly shrilled and the maths teacher jumped up and left the room. In the midst of this pandemonium I set about fixing six posters to the wall. The students, meanwhile, showed unmistakable signs of confusion in the presence of three different teachers. As if they didn't know which was in charge and might suddenly start ordering them about. Finally, the other teachers left, I switched on a tape of soft meditative music, played on the pipes of Pan. A different and calmer atmosphere settled on the room. After a couple of minutes, when everyone had calmed down, I faded the music out. Before I could speak, one of the students struck up a conversation:

Student *I know what we are going to do.*
Teacher *Do you?*
Student *Yes, we speak about I.*
Teacher *About you?*
Student *No, not about me. I mean about everybody myself.*

The teacher now spoke to the whole class, asking them to look at the symbolic pictures he had just put up (Fig. 7.1). After a while he said: 'You see all the materials? I'd like you to get together in groups of equal size. Choose a poster and stand right in front of it. You can play with words. Stick pictures on the poster, write words, and draw. It's better if you don't talk a lot!' He gestured towards the sheets of paper, cards, scissors, pens, magazines and glue set out on a table.

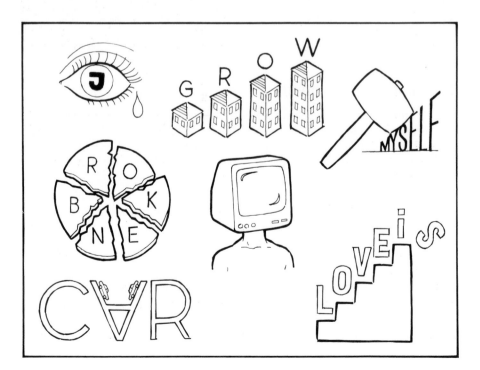

Figure 7.1

3 Creating posters and poems

Stimulated by the music, the students began working. The teacher broke in briefly: 'Concentrate on the *drawing* on your poster. On the cards write the words that come to your mind when you look at your poster. Stick them on the poster anywhere you like. You can also *write* on the poster, or draw, or cut pictures out of the magazines and stick them on – whatever you want. I think it's better not to ask questions.'

He then started the music again.

Figures 7.2 and 7.3 Students working on their posters

Gradually the process of shaping the posters created a powerfully motivating dynamic. The more developed the posters became, the more creativity they evoked. This came out clearly in the extract from what one student wrote about this stage in the final evaluation on page 93.

From time to time the students stood back from their posters to look at what they had done and to form an impression of it. The teacher did not intervene in any way.

As groups finished their posters, the teacher gave them time to look at others' posters and to watch other groups who were still working. This began the transition from the movement and spontaneity involved in creating the posters to the state of calm and reflection needed for poem writing.

The teacher asked the students to react to their own posters in the form of a poem. He reminded them of the free structure of the children's poems on the display board.

The writing of poems took up most of the last fifteen minutes or so of this lesson.

4 Ending the lesson / Concealing the poems

Before ending the lesson, the teacher asked the students to sign their poems. Interestingly, their feelings of authorship and identification with their work were so strong that not one student signed their sheet at the top as they normally did at school.

While this was going on, the teacher handed out envelopes and asked each student to put their poem into one *but without marking the envelope in any way*. The teacher then collected the envelopes and kept them until the next lesson.

The students involved in this trial lesson seemed to be reassured by the fact that their poems were thus carefully kept from public scrutiny at this stage. We had, however, asked the students if it was OK if we published their poems later on. One of their poems is shown in Figure 7.4.

MYSELF

I am poor,
I have no friends,
No love!
Who could help me,
that I am not be alone?
Happyness is far away!
In all my dreams
I look for love,
but I don't find!
Then I weep,
and nobody can consoles me!
Every day I can see black
I am lonly.
I want a friend,
a friend, a friend!
Why just am I alone?
If I think about this,
some tears run down my face!
Would you be me friend,
I need you!
Then I'm going to be happy
and I have not reason, to weep!
You need love
all members need love,
I would be quiete,
if you tell me something
and I wouldn't disturb you!
Please be my friend –
I need you.

Figure 7.4

5 Reading others' poems

It is sometimes quite difficult to establish links in theme and content between lessons that take place some days apart. In the trial class we used the same instrumental music in the next lesson as in the first in order to re-evoke the mood in which the posters and poems had been created.

With this music in the background the teacher handed out the sealed envelopes containing the poems and told the students to hand back the envelope with the poem inside if they happened to get their own. Excitement began to build as students realised what was happening – that not only was someone else going to be reading their poem but they were going to be reading someone else's. The suspense seemed to heighten their alertness and contribute enormously to their involvement and motivation.

They opened the envelopes and read the poems in silence.

6 Emotional feedback

A recent approach to working with literature in school classrooms is to read a text not in the light of an expert's (probably the teacher's) interpretation of it, but rather to encourage personal interpretations. The teacher then tries to elaborate and refine all these individual interpretations by staging activities which encourage students to compare and contrast their interpretation with those of their colleagues and otherwise discuss and think about them.

It was in the spirit of this approach that the teacher said: 'Write a letter to the poem's author. Write down what you think about the text, what you feel when you read it. It will be interesting for the writer to learn what you like about his or her poem. Feel free to criticise it, too.'

The students then each wrote a letter and gave it to the author of the poem they had read. One such letter is shown in Figure 7.5 and relates to the poem in Figure 7.4.

Dear Monika !!!

I think your text is very expressive. Your text gives me not a good feeling. I know you have a big problem and sometimes I have this problem too. I think you need not weep. I think you have enough friends. You are a lovely girl and I like you very much.

Sabi

Figure 7.5

Meanwhile, the teacher cleared the display board to make way for the class's poems which were then pinned up for all to see. Then after the authors had had time to read and think about the letters they had received, everyone was free to stand up, move around and talk to both to the student whose poem they had read and to the one who had given them a letter.

Comment: As these examples indicate, the students reacted to the poems seriously. Additionally, since they actually did have something to say to the authors, they saw this writing task as having a real and vivid communicative purpose.

Students should be free, of course, to withhold their work from 'publication', but in our experience when an atmosphere of trust has been developed, few ever do.

7 Evaluation

Our experiences in doing units like this have convinced us that they not only deepen students' understanding and appreciation of literary texts in general, but that they also give them useful insights into processes whereby they themselves can create real pieces of art. To facilitate such growth in perspective, the teacher concluded this unit by asking his students to produce a written evaluation of it and what they had experienced. Figure 7.6 shows a typical expression of how enjoyable practically all the participants found this work.

> My lovelist lesson.
> At first we got posters with topics. We stuck them on the wall and Mr Puchta gave us felt pens. Now he switched on the cassette recorder. It was a good music to feel about the topic. The topic of our group was "J". And now we wrote feeling-words and things witch we tought on the poster. I think that was the best English lesson, because we were able to wrote our feelings on the poster, but the ideas about poetry was also good. We wrote the poetry also out from our topic. Now the poems are hanging on the wall in our class, so that each pupil could read them. I hope we will make more "super-lessons". The lesson was good for myself, so J think.

Figure 7.6

Another student wrote:

In the beginning I felt not good. I couldn't think about words, but ten minutes later I had written and written and I didn't knew when to stop. This was a good feeling . . .

This is typical for the first time we try a unit like this. Students may well have no confidence in their abilities to create anything at all. However, these abilities do not lie far beneath the surface.

CONCLUDING DISCUSSION

Teachers have frequently asked us how we introduce the idea of poems and get a class working. Actually, in the trial class, students set to work on their poems in a matter-of-fact manner with very little in the way of stage management on the teacher's part. An important factor here was probably the amount of careful preparation leading up to the creative writing phase. A display of poems had been prepared and students had had an opportunity to see what was there; in Stage 1 the teacher had sensitised her students to aspects of poetry which go beyond the stereotypical features of rhyme and rhythm, such as personalisation of content. The purpose of Stage 3 was to build an atmosphere conducive to creativity. Finally, the teacher was working within an overall approach designed to foster students' confidence in their abilities to express themselves generally.

Suggested texts

The following are good sources of children's poems for inclusion on the display board described in Stage 1:

Blishen, E (ed) *The School that I'd Like* Penguin Books Ltd 1969
Cadbury's Book of Children's Poetry Beaver Books 1987
Duff, A *That's Life* CUP 1979
Godwin, N (ed) *Families and Friends, Town Life in Story, Poem and Picture* O'Brien Educational 1978
Grossman, F *Getting from Here to There: Writing and Reading Poetry* Boynton/Cook 1982
Linkletter, A *Kids Say the Darndest Things* Prentice-Hall 1957
Moskowitz, G *Caring and Sharing in the Foreign Language Class* Newbury House 1978
Opie, I and P *The Lore and Language of Schoolchildren* OUP 1959
Koch, K *Rose Where Did You Get That Red?* Random House 1973
Swan, M *Kaleidoscope* CUP 1979 and *Spectrum* CUP 1978
Shaw, F *You Know Me Aunty Nelly?* Wolfe 1970

The theatre of the absurd

Creating an understanding of absurdity – in everyday life and on stage

---

LEVEL

Upper intermediate +

TIME

3–5 hours

TRIAL CLASS

Twenty-six seventeen- to eighteen-year-olds in their eighth year of English; three fifty-minute lessons a week

AIMS

Making literature personally relevant to students; encouraging students to talk about their view of their life and their place in the world; developing a literary theory from the students' own insights; sensitising learners to the difference between content and process in groupwork

Language areas and skills

Reading; analysing and discussing literary texts; vocabulary linked to text

Materials

Stage 1:   Hand-out of reading text ('Samuel Beckett in the "Age of Godot"', Fig. 8.1, p. 98)
Stage 3:   Note cards or pieces of paper
Stage 5:   Blu-tack or Sellotape, large sheets of paper
Stages 6–7: Large sheets of paper
Stage 8:   Audio-recording of *Waiting for Godot*; selection of works by Beckett; reading passage from *Waiting for Godot*; Task Cards A, B, C (Figs. 8.2–8.4, pp. 101–2); OHP transparencies; observation sheet (Fig. 8.6, p. 103)
Stage 10:   Small pieces of paper
Stage 11:   Hand-outs summarising discussion (Fig. 8.11, p. 108)

BACKGROUND AND RATIONALE

One of our aims in planning the sequence of activities we describe below was to find a way of developing an aspect of literary theory from students' insights. We believed that this could only have the effect of encouraging students to think more broadly and independently about other works of literature they might read later on their own.

The topic we settled on was Samuel Beckett and the theatre of the absurd. We decided to begin with a secondary text (a text about a text) in our trial class, since texts of this sort are sometimes found in advanced coursebooks. Also, the text we chose – because it touched both on the writer and his work – seemed to offer a general introduction to the topic.

Another reason we chose this text is that many teachers like working with texts of this sort for the following reasons: (1) they often appear in coursebooks and supplementary materials with ready-made notes on current events (here the commemoration of Beckett's seventy-fifth birthday); (2) they often cover a wide topic in a compact form; and (3) they typically come with glossaries. In fact, trainee teachers in Austria are often asked to work with secondary texts by their trainers who feel that they are easier for an untrained teacher to work with because of the commentary that is supplied. Unfortunately, secondary texts tend to be rather dry compared with the literature they deal with. However, it occurred to us that using a text that seemed rather flat on the surface, would be a good test of our method.

UNIT SUMMARY

1 Preparation
Hand out the text 'Samuel Beckett in the "Age of Godot"' some days before starting the unit in class.

Lesson 1

2 Creating an absurd situation
Begin the first lesson by behaving absurdly.

3 Collection of impressions
Students note down their impressions on cards.

4 Categorising impressions
In groups, the students swap cards, discuss, and categorise them.

5 Presentation of analyses
The groups present their findings by arranging their cards on large sheets of paper or producing mind maps. Summarise the students' reactions on the board.

Lesson 2

6 Analysing the text

In small groups the students read excerpts from the text and analyse them using the categories *Facts*, *Thoughts*, and *Reasons*.

Lesson 3

7 The groundwork for theory

Collect the results of the groupwork and present them on a poster or on the board. Elicit a summary of the characteristics of the theatre of the absurd.

8 Experiencing literature

8.1 Content-oriented groupwork

Students work in small groups on different tasks. Some scan complete works, some read more closely, and some listen to representative passages.

8.2 Process-oriented groupwork

A 'process' observer sits with each of the content-oriented literature groups.

Lesson 4

9 Process evaluation

The process observers report. Discussion follows.

10 Content evaluation

Students from the content groups present their findings.

Lesson 5

11 Discussing the ideas expressed in the texts

Using the findings of the groups, along with conclusions from the discussion in Stage 7, elicit and discuss the ideas behind the theatre of the absurd.

12 Reflecting on everyday experience

Students discuss the ways in which their everyday life, including school life, is absurd.

1 Preparation

The text we chose is reproduced on page 98. We noticed immediately that it does nothing to explain or exemplify absurdity, a key element of its topic. In particular, the writer approaches this issue in a way we thought unlikely to connect with our students' own worlds of experience. Because of this we decided to introduce the text in a way that got them to experience absurdity first-hand.

Following institutional tradition we handed the text out to the students a few days before the planned in-class exploitation and asked them to read it, using a dictionary when necessary.

2 Creating an absurd situation

The beginning of the lesson seemed an ideal time to stage our planned experience of absurdity since classes tend to commence in a ritualised fashion. We hit on the plan of having the teacher go against his established ritual in every respect possible.

The teacher commented:

I didn't find it at all easy to behave absurdly in the introductory phase. What would the students think? Normally I take great care to establish rapport. But today I behaved totally differently. My 'Good evening' when I walked into the class – it was morning – didn't really seem to bother my students. Were they at all aware of this greeting ritual? 'What an interesting service,' I said as I approached my desk. This had them pricking up their ears. 'Where is the captain?' I asked next. Now they looked really surprised. 'Oh, hello. You're under the car,' I said next, without addressing anyone directly, behaving as if I was surprised. I could see that they were getting more and more perplexed. 'I'm hungry,' I added. Some of the students were now looking thoroughly flummoxed. In order to stop anyone offering me their lunch I quickly asked, 'Is this the bar?' At this, there was some laughter and despite myself I almost joined in. I wheeled round and out of the blue addressed one student, 'A drink? I'm thirsty.' He was completely lost for words. 'Where is your teddy bear?' I asked another student. I was in the groove now. It was fun. The rest of the class looked at the student and roared with laughter. I took advantage of the fact that attention had been momentarily diverted away from me and picked up the class register, linking in to the familiar ritual. 'Oh, the memorial stone for the dead,' I said as I reached my desk. I am quite sure the students had no idea what I was trying to get across to them. But then why should they comprehend absurdity? I relaxed and opened the register. 'Where's Godot?' I asked. An aha-look crossed the faces of one or two students. Or was I just imagining this? 'Is he missing?' I continued – just a bit glad that that absurd game of mine had thus come to an end.

Of course, it was difficult for students to interpret such odd behaviour in a teacher. But now it was a matter of getting them to recall their reactions of astonishment, perplexity, and incomprehension.

Samuel Beckett in the "Age of Godot"

BECKETT, who was born near Dublin in 1906, celebrated his 75th birthday on April 13. Winner of the Nobel Prize for Literature in 1969, the Irish author is generally considered the world's greatest living playwright.

The 1953 premiere of his "Waiting for Godot" in Paris provoked an outcry and turned a new page in the history of Western drama. Ironically, the most erudite of all 20th-century playwrights delivered the coup de grace to Aristotelian aesthetics, a death blow that became all the more apparent with each subsequent work. Theater as a genre will never be the same because Samuel Beckett lived and wrote, and even though current trends in both mainstream and avant-garde drama have moved away from Beckett's model, all living writers owe him an enormous debt.

LIKE T.S. Eliot's "The Waste Land," which communicated the anguish of the lost generation after World War I, "Waiting for Godot" captured the spirit of its age, an age of existential alienation and metaphysical gloom spawned in the sorrow of World War II. Side by side, these two literary landmarks sum up human experience in the 20th century, and they will remain the moral touchstones of our world, the two single works that convey most deeply what it means to be alive in our fretful time. Not surprisingly, many cultural historians refer to the post-World War II period as the "age of Godot."

In this play, against a blasted and desolate landscape, two vaudeville tramps perform a series of music-hall turns to while away the livelong day waiting for Godot, whose arrival, they presume, will justify their lives. But Godot never comes, and the two tramps begin to doubt their own existence. Still, they keep on waiting, caught in a meaningless cycle of eternal returns.

With these two, inspired by the great silent film comics, Beckett created the perfect dramatic vehicle for phenomenological futility. He gave the philosophy of the absurd a human face. He also gave modern drama a whole new bag of tricks that enabled it to express the pain born of Hiroshima and the Holocaust.

BECKETT ultimately banished from the theater all its traditional supports — plot, character and dialogue. Similar to the reductionism of the Abstract Expressionist painters, Beckett's aesthetic is non-representational and non-objective. Although the theme of his work never varies — his plays always stare fixedly into the empty center of human existence — his command over his technique has through the years become more and more dazzling.

Beckett is a minimalist. He has ruthlessly stripped away all externals from the stage in order to discover drama in the undramatic. He has made his language more and more sparing in order to discover poetry in the prosaic. In terms of economy, the quintessential Beckett play is "Breath," which lasts only a few seconds and consists only of sounds — a single cry and breathing in and out, but structured in such a way as to present an aural metaphor for the brevity of the human life cycle beginning with a puking wail and ending, not with a death rattle but a sigh of relief.

Beckett's interest in technique has led him to experiment with all forms of dramatic expression. He has written script for radio, television and film. He always exploits the specific potentiality of each medium fully. For example, "Cascando," a radio play, cannot be done any other way since the nature of the writing depends on the absence of images.

In contrast, a new work written for Stuttgart television (to be aired next June) has no dialogue whatsoever. It is a dramatic interplay of color, movement and sound. Beckett himself has directed many of his plays to great effect, including a recent and memorable "Happy Days" in London with Billie Whitelaw and what some critics consider the definitive "Waiting for Godot" in Berlin.

ALTHOUGH Beckett is most widely known for his plays, his career has encompassed virtually all modes of literature: poetry, novels, short stories and critical studies. His most recent novel in French, "Mal Vu, Mal Dit" was published on April 1 by Les Éditions de Minuit. "Company," which appeared last year, is the author's latest and, for many, his finest novel in English.

A man lying on his back in pitch darkness imagines that he hears a voice talking to him — the com-

pany of the title. But by the end, silence conquers all, and the nameless, faceless anti-hero remains as he was in the beginning, as he is and always shall be. Alone. Although the book has the usual dosage of sardonic humor and bitter despair, it strikes a new note of lyricism and tenderness, and in it Beckett gives us a series of vignettes more autobiographical than he has ever granted us before.

But technique alone does not begin to explain the power and fascination Beckett's work exerts. First and foremost, he is a master craftsman of language, a great poet who is able to play tricks with words in a way only Shakespeare, Dickens and Joyce have done.

Beckett received a classical education. And it shows in every line he writes; the panoply of rhetorical devices lurking beneath the seemingly simple surface of his prose staggers the critical imagination. But the secret key to the beauty of Beckett's style is rhythm. The cadences of his sentences are unforgettable. Nowhere is this more apparent than in "Rockaby" which will also be presented at the Festival d'Automne in Paris.

THE PLAY is a duet between an old woman and her own voice as she rocks herself to death — a forlorn icon of absolute human isolation. Once again, Beckett juxtaposes images of the womb and the tomb. Instead of waiting for Godot, rocking has now become the central metaphor for human life. The old theme of the existential quest remains, but Beckett's language has never been either more humble or more beautiful. Almost every word is a simple Anglo-Saxon monosyllable, but they create an hallucinatory incantation which is both a lullaby and a dirge.

"Performing Beckett," remarked Estelle Parsons, the Academy Award-winning American actress, "was one of the great joys of my professional life. Along with Shakespeare, he presents an actor with all possible difficulties and all possible rewards."

Winnie in "Happy Days" keeps mumbling to herself half-forgotten lines of great poetry that surface in her mind. She thanks God for the classics because, even in a tattered state, they "help one through the day."

Beckett has become a living classic and has helped contemporary man get through the second half of the 20th century. By taking the form of the farce and infusing it with full tragic significance, he has provided the modern world with its only possible catharsis in which humor as well as pity and terror reconcile us to life. His words act for us.

(AM.) - ARTHUR HOLMBERG IN THE INTERNATIONAL HERALD TRIBUNE

Figure 8.1

Arthur Holmberg, *International Herald Tribune*, April 1981

3 Collection of impressions

Without actually telling the students what the aim of Stage 2 was, the teacher now elicited and pooled expressions of what people had felt about it. First, he handed out cards and asked the students to jot down their impressions on them anonymously.

He stressed to the class that it was very important for them to have a bit of quiet thinking time before they jotted down their impressions. (Students are often not used to such quiet phases, so teachers should take care to give them sufficient time to actually form and note down detailed recollections – not just a half a minute or so but three to five minutes.) After this reflection time, the teacher asked the students to put their cards face down on their desks for collection. As we thought that most of these impressions would be of an emotional nature, we thought that getting them down on paper would help clarify them and show the difference between their expectations of what would happen in the lesson and what actually did happen. We saw this as an essential introduction to the subject of absurdity.

Here are some of the impressions written on the cards:

It was crazy, lesson is extraordinary, no sense, nonsense, astonishment, feeling of confusion, strange, silly, silly person, lesson is not happiness, humour, funny, entertaining, black humour, surprised, extraordinary, grotesque, unrealistic, ex- aggerated, senseless, surrealistic, absurd, comic, totally changed situation, fun/ good, S = clown, phantastic/stupid, depressing, feeling of being teased, stupid, good language experiment, GB has lost a great actor with Mr S, simple normal madness, excited, enjoyed the situation, smile and be happy.

These notes served as as basis for analysis in the following stage.

4 Categorising impressions

The aim of this stage was to analyse the students' impressions for simi- larities and contrasts.

The teacher put students in groups of about five. He gave each group cards he had collected previously, saying: 'Look at the cards. These are some students' impressions. I'm sure you can put them in different groups somehow.'

In some classes, particularly when the level of English is a bit lower, you will need to guide students more explicitly about criteria for ca- tegorising, for example, personal reactions/feelings, contents and interpretation.

Naturally, the groups were supposed to work in English. In upper-level classes like ours this is seldom a problem.

5 Presentation of analyses

After categorising the individual impressions, the groups presented their findings to the whole class. As presentation aids, some groups stuck their cards on a large sheet of paper. Other groups, instead of using the cards themselves, drew mind maps. In both cases, the groups referred to their posters during their presentations. After the presentations, the teacher drew things together by pointing out cases where groups reached similar conclusions or categorisations or strikingly different ones.

Comment: The group presentations and the teacher's summary were intended to help the students to reflect more vividly on their own and others' experiences of absurd situations. And this reflection, we hoped, would help the students to make sense of the text 'Samuel Beckett in the "Age of Godot" '.

6 Analysing the text

Since a detailed analysis of the whole text would obviously take a long time, the teacher assigned different blocks of the text to different groups of three students each. The teacher asked each group to make notes, on a large sheet of paper, under three headings: *Facts in the text* (What is said in your paragraph?), *Personal thoughts* (What occurs to you when you think about these facts?), *Reasons for thoughts* (Why do these thoughts come to mind?). If students are not used to approaching a text in this way, the result at first can be a bit rough. Even so, it is important to begin encouraging students to read with greater awareness of a text's effects on their thoughts and emotions – and most students soon get better at separating what they read in a text from what the text makes them think of.

7 The groundwork for theory

The teacher now elicited the different groups' findings and put them together under the three headings on large sheets of paper. This was in order to begin the move from the students' own views towards a deeper consideration of Beckett's work in the following stage.

8 Experiencing literature

The plan was to confront the class with a number of pieces by Samuel Beckett in a way which would foster independence in approaching his work.

8.1 Content-oriented groupwork
The teacher divided the class into three 'content' groups, spaced as far away from each other as possible. Each group received different tasks.

This was not only so that more of Beckett's work could be looked at in the short period of time available, but also, and equally importantly, in order to create opportunities for cooperative interaction. In addition to these groups, the teacher created a fourth, 'process evaluation' group whose role is described later in 8.2 (p.103). First, here is what each of the three *content groups* did in our trial class.

Group A

Group A got a cassette recorder and a recorded passage from *Waiting for Godot*. We had selected a passage we thought was (a) typical of the work as a whole, (b) gave a fair picture of the literary merits of the play, and (c) was not too demanding. This passage starts on page 12 of the 1956 Faber and Faber paperback edition with 'VLADIMIR: Where was I . . .' and ends with 'ESTRAGON: I had a dream.' on page 15. The tasks shown on Task Card A (Fig. 8.2) were designed to encourage listening for gist.

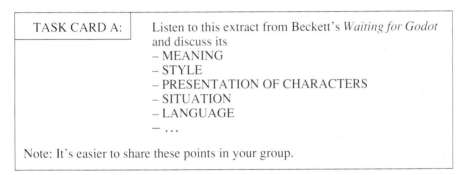

TASK CARD A:	Listen to this extract from Beckett's *Waiting for Godot* and discuss its – MEANING – STYLE – PRESENTATION OF CHARACTERS – SITUATION – LANGUAGE – ...
Note: It's easier to share these points in your group.	

Figure 8.2

Group B

Group B received a selection of books containing whole works by Beckett. Task Card B (Fig. 8.3) indicates general features students had to skim for. The main aim here was simply to give some members of the class the opportunity to see and hold the actual books, since physical encounter with works of literature is an experience not to be underestimated in its importance for getting students to read these works on their own out of interest. Additionally, this kind of broad, preliminary contact is also extremely important in enabling students to form an impression of a writer's style and the overall structure of a work. However, this skim reading was by no means meant to take the place of intensive reading. This was to come later on.

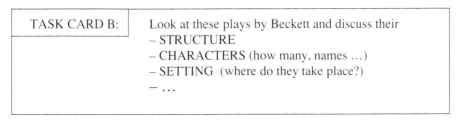

TASK CARD B:	Look at these plays by Beckett and discuss their – STRUCTURE – CHARACTERS (how many, names ...) – SETTING (where do they take place?) – ...

Figure 8.3

Group C

Group C were given a reading passage from *Waiting for Godot*. Again we chose a passage typical of the text as a whole, but interesting and not too difficult linguistically. This passage followed on from the passage given to Group A, running from page 16 to 19 of the same edition (from 'VLADIMIR: Don't tell me!' to 'VLADIMIR: At his horse.'). They also received a task card (Fig. 8.4) to help focus their reading on particular aspects of the text.

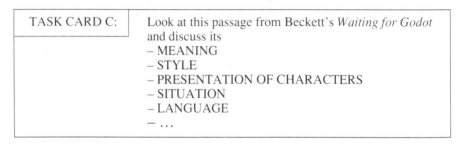

| TASK CARD C: | Look at this passage from Beckett's *Waiting for Godot* and discuss its
– MEANING
– STYLE
– PRESENTATION OF CHARACTERS
– SITUATION
– LANGUAGE
– ... |

Figure 8.4

The teacher asked the students in each group to record their findings on OHP transparencies so that they could share them with the whole class later (in Stage 10).

Note: If there are more than about fifteen students in the class, you can make more than three groups and either give some groups the same task or have the extra groups working with new passages in ways similar to those indicated on Task Cards A and C.

Figure 8.5
Students in
Group A
during
groupwork

8.2 Process-oriented groupwork

The fourth group (i.e. the 'process evaluation' group) consisted of three students, each of whom had the job of *observing* one of the three content groups at work.

The teacher gave each member of this group a hand-out to guide them in observing how the 'content' people interacted, what they did, and how they expressed themselves. The teacher took particular care to stress that the observers were not 'deputy teachers' and that their observations were not in any way going to be used to determine anyone's grade.

The observation sheet (Fig. 8.6) reflects, in its fourth section, our experience that observation and evaluation work best if observers are encouraged not simply to record what they see but to identify with the group they are observing as much as possible.

OBSERVATION CHART: Join one group and watch them work under the following points:	
INTERACTION Conflicts/cooperation/ isolation/… Anything else?	

ACTIVITIES
How is work done?
Intensity of activities
    and individual
        working arrangements	

LANGUAGE USED English/German/ Fluency/problems	
OBSERVER'S FEELINGS Would you like to work with this group? Why (not)? Describe your feelings.	

Figure 8.6

9 Process evaluation

After the 'content' groups had finished working through their task cards, the three observers briefly came together and shared their observations. They then reported to the whole class. This led to a very interesting discussion both of language and the social aspects of the groupwork.

10 Content evaluation

Next, the students in the 'content' groups made oral presentations, with reference to OHP transparencies of their notes.

Presentations of this sort are sometimes difficult to manage. Some students in the 'audience' tend to lean back and switch off. If this happens, the reporting phase becomes tedious for everyone. In order to stimulate the listeners to actively participate, the teacher distributed comments on slips of paper. The messages on the slips (Figure 8.7) were intended to provoke interest and comment.

Figure 8.7

The teacher had prepared these slips during the previous stages and had fitted them to particular students and how they seemed to be reacting. It was very important here to strike the right tone, since messages like these are unlikely to work if students perceive them as commands. What you can say to one student you cannot say to another, so you need to know your class fairly well at this stage. However, the stimuli shown here seemed to work well with this class. Figures 8.8–8.10 summarise what the 'content' groups came up with.

GROUP A:

listened to an extract from Beckett's *Waiting for Godot*, pp. 21–15 (to '. . . I had a dream.')

Meaning
relation to Bible: Vladimir explains to Estragon the situation in the Bible – whether two thieves have been damned to hell or have been saved by God

Style
dialogue form: question–answer / expressive style / fast rhythm / everyday language: not composed / no abstractions – simple, clear – dramatic effect

Characters
Estragon: ignorant, not religious, forgets everything
Vladimir: educated, explains the situation to Estragon

Situation
– two tramps are quarrelling, they go on waiting for Godot who should save them from death of hell
– they then go waiting for Godot at a tree that has no leaves. And they again quarrel whether it is a tree or a bush. They waited yesterday, today, tomorrow and so on
– then they stop talking and one of them wants to sleep but the other does not allow him to do so
– a sort of impasse – no way out of this depressing situation

Language
– reduced . . . dialogue, language of despairing resignation and hopelessness, and language of quarrelling
– they sometimes talk at cross-purposes
– he uses not only language but also musical elements

Figure 8.8

GROUP B:

looked at three plays by Beckett and discussed them, viz. *Waiting for Godot, Endgame, All That Fall*

	Godot	*Endgame*	*All That Fall*
Structure	tragic comedy in two acts – radio play dialogue form	play in one act radio play dialogue form	radio play strong, vivid dialogue form – one act
Characters	Estragon Vladimir Lucky / Pozzo A boy (5 persons)	Hamm Clov Nagg Nell (4 persons)	Mrs Rooney / Christy / Mr Tyler / Stocum / Tommy / Mr Barrel / Miss Fitt / Doll / Mr Rooney (10 persons)
Setting	country road	dark, grey room closed curtains	country railway station, rural sounds
Main ideas	metaphor about the nature of human life, modern morality play		

Figure 8.9

GROUP C:

looked at a passage from Beckett's *Waiting for Godot*, pp. 16–19
(NB: continuation of Group A's extract)

Meaning
situation of despair, hopelessness, problem of hanging on, Vladimir and Estragon commenting on Godot – Estragon on Vladimir

Style
very short dialogues, many stage directions
many passages of ironic/black humour, many repetitions
difficult language

Presentation of characters
Vladimir is an optimist; wants to wait for Godot
Estragon: hopeless pessimist, has given up, wants to commit suicide immediately

Situation
conflict between Estragon and Vladimir

Language
reduced language, no complete sentences, but not colloquial

Figure 8.10

These summaries clearly show how many of the critical issues were noted by the students themselves. In fact, they cover the basics of Beckett's work and the theatre of the absurd pretty well. Again, the teacher had not lectured and had given out no subject matter hand-outs.

11 Discussing the ideas expressed in the texts

The class, in plenary, talked about the ideas expressed in the literature of the theatre of the absurd and how these ideas were expressed. The teacher acted as facilitator by unobtrusively adding relevant background information to points brought up by the students.

Some of the ideas discussed were:
- the sense of man's alienation
- the cruelty of existence
- the futility of conventional objectives
- the futility of man's struggle
- the strong vein of fantasy

The teacher recorded the results of this stage later and worked them into hand-outs (see Fig. 8.11: 'Common Factors of the Absurd' and 'Points Looked For'), so that the students had a reference for later study and revision.

12 Reflecting on everyday experience

A work of literature can be gripping, even in the classroom, if students find it contains reflections of their own everyday life and experience. It can be more gripping still if they realise that they can read literature not simply for diversion or to take in facts (as for an exam) but to enhance and, perhaps, even restructure their perceptions of reality. And so the teacher began this final stage of the unit by reminding his students of the feelings and experiences they had had in the very first, 'absurd' stage. He then asked the class to spend a few minutes thinking silently about what they found absurd in their own lives. This led afterwards to lively, and at times emotional, discussion. The notes in Figure 8.11 ('The Absurd in our Personal Everyday Lives') show the gist of this final activity.

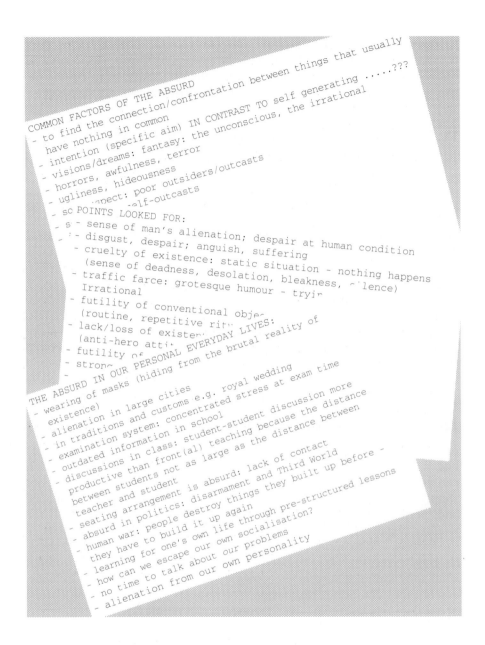

COMMON FACTORS OF THE ABSURD
- to find the connection/confrontation between things that usually have nothing in common
- intention (specific aim) IN CONTRAST TO self generating .....???
- visions/dreams: fantasy: the unconscious, the irrational
- horrors, awfulness, terror
- ugliness, hideousness
- ..spect: poor outsiders/outcasts
- sc POINTS LOOKED FOR: -elf-outcasts
- s - sense of man's alienation; despair at human condition
- .'- disgust, despair; anguish, suffering
- cruelty of existence: static situation - nothing happens
  (sense of deadness, desolation, bleakness, ~'lence)
- traffic farce: grotesque humour - tryir
  Irrational
- futility of conventional obje-
  (routine, repetitive rit~
- lack/loss of existen~
  (anti-hero atti+   EVERYDAY LIVES:
- futility o~   PERSONAL   the brutal reality of
- stron~   IN OUR   (hiding from
THE ABSURD
- wearing of masks
  existence)
- alienation in large cities
- in traditions and customs e.g. royal wedding
- examination system: concentrated stress at exam time
- outdated information in school
- discussions in class: student-student discussion more
  productive than front(al) teaching because the distance
  between students not as large as the distance between
  teacher and student
- seating arrangement is absurd: lack of contact
- absurd in politics: disarmament and Third World
- human war: people destroy things they built up before -
  they have to build it up again
- learning for one's own life through pre-structured lessons
- how can we escape our own socialisation?
- no time to talk about our own problems
- alienation from our own personality

Figure 8.11

CONCLUDING DISCUSSION

Literature is well known as a stimulant to sentiment and reverie. Additionally, for old and young readers alike, its power to stimulate curiosity in one's own life, identity, surroundings gives it considerable potential to motivate growth and change. It seems, though, increasingly difficult to get students interested in reading the classics. The impact of TV, film and video on the reading habits of young people in particular is notorious (as are its profound and widespread consequences on teaching and learning in general). In our view, the competition from the modern visual media makes it absolutely vital that teachers attempting to use literature should place great weight on enhancing the learning atmosphere in their classrooms, on involving their students in active learning and on bridging the gap between the world of a writer and that of their students. We believe that this is the only viable alternative to just giving up on literature in the foreign (or native) language class.

We are certainly not proposing that teachers abandon the classics and teach instead some kind of 'literature for the masses' with heavy doses of sentimentality and sensationalism. What we are advocating is a general attempt to link language learning to the processes of growth in the personal identity of young people and to take account of: (1) their need for learning materials to have personal significance, (2) the importance of arousing their curiosity, and (3) the importance of dealing with issues of conflict. The use of literature, especially quality literature, is in many ways ideally suited for this enterprise. Good literature is, for one thing, much richer than bad literature in the range of feelings, views, kinds of behaviour and situations it portrays. However, it may help to choose literature read by young people of similar ages in English-speaking countries. The problems and concerns are more likely to be similar but with an intriguingly different perspective. As one student recently remarked to us, 'I don't want to read about pensioners. I don't want to read about middle-aged people . . .'

Basically, teachers need to explore ways of encouraging learners to 'take literature in', not as if they were empty vessels, but rather as whole people, and to enter into this or that imaginative world. For this to happen, learners must be able to see connections between their own world and that of the writer – their routes to new destinations need to be lined with landmarks. As Ruth Cohn once put it (1981, p. 166): 'Almost any topic can be of interest to learners provided they have some means of relating to it and haven't just bumped into it like some object in the dark.' We hope we have shown how a topic as remote (probably) as the theatre of the absurd can be linked to the world of young language learners.

Suggested reading

Bassnett, S and Grundy, P *Language through Literature* Longman 1993

Carter, R and Long, MN *The Web of Words: Exploring Literature Through Language* CUP 1987

Collie, J and Slater, J *Literature in the Language Classroom: A Resource Book of Ideas and Activities* CUP 1987

Maley, A and Duff, A *The Inward Ear: Poetry in the Language Classroom* CUP 1989

Maley, A and Moulding, S *Poem into Poem: Reading and Writing Poems with Students of English* CUP 1985

Tomlinson, B *Openings* Lingual House 1986

Text workshop with CALL

First steps into the world of word processing

LEVEL
Intermediate – upper intermediate

TIME
A four-day special course with four forty-five minute lessons per day

TRIAL CLASS
Twelve fourteen-year-olds in their fourth year of learning English

AIMS
Making CALL part of humanistic language learning; familiarising students with hardware and word-processing software; highlighting writing as a process and downplaying writing as a product

Language areas and skills
Use of computers and word-processing software; listening; speaking; writing; reading

Materials
Stage 2: Simple software (e.g. Zavatex); floppy disks
Stage 4: Hand-out of diagram (Fig. 9.1, p. 116)
Stage 5: OHP; cut-up pictures from picture story (Figs. 9.2–9.7, pp. 117–21); a piece of paper with a very small hole in; sentences from story cut up on separate pieces of paper (Fig. 9.8, p. 121); skeleton text on large sheet of paper (p. 122)
Stage 6: Blu-tack; model text to read out (p. 124); soft music
Stage 7: Four texts for dictation
Stage 8: Four copies of text for dictation
Stage 9: Hand-outs of mini-sagas (p. 129)
Stage 11: Paper; scissors; glue

BACKGROUND AND RATIONALE

Faith seems to have been growing lately that the computer will bring about a revolution in the foreign language classroom and that students' problems with accuracy and vocabulary learning, as well as those of low motivation, have at last found their remedy. A critical look at most CALL software, however, suggests the reverse. For one thing, drill-and-practice software seems to predominate, and this is nothing less than a revival of old-style programmed learning or, in the words of Christian Holzmann, 'drill and kill'.

Teachers in favour of working with such programs frequently point out their students' high motivation to use them and suggest that this alone is sufficient reason to turn on the machine. But plainly motivation isn't enough of a justification. After all, a great many people, not least teenagers, are easily captivated by gambling machines, whose pedagogical value we nevertheless doubt. There is also good reason to believe that this motivation tends to be short-lived and is prone to fade rapidly when the computer is a fixture in other school subjects too.

There are, to be sure, programs that can foster improvement in the target language, especially programs involving the reconstruction of texts (e.g. Quartext by Higgins and Johnson). These programs help learners to develop an awareness of the features of good text, in particular cohesion and coherence. There are also a few good simulation programs for involving learners in communicative interactions, with the computer being mainly a source of stimuli.

Generally though, CALL and humanistic teaching/learning have so far seemed to be two very different things. At least, it is far from obvious how to integrate regular use of computers into language learning without violating the basic principles of humanistic learning – especially the importance accorded to non-superficial human interaction.

However, one area in language teaching where we think the computer can be very helpful is writing, a skill sadly neglected in many foreign language classrooms and not least in communicative and humanistic ones. As Brooks and Grundy have observed:

Our culture typically chooses to forget that writing is to do with mastering a process. Instead, we think of (and value) writing only as a product – so that the 'perfect' poem or completed essay are held up as though they were all that writing is. So it's hardly a surprise that more or less all the teaching materials for serious or more advanced learners treat writing as the analysis and subsequent imitation of a model text. And it's easy to see why the teaching of reading and writing, when seen as text based activities, have not appealed to the humanistic movement.

A Brooks and P Grundy, *Designer Writing: Principles and Practices for Advanced Level Writing Classes*, Pilgrims 1988 p. 5

One common feature of product-oriented writing is judging learners by the number of errors they make. For example, writing figures prominently in testing. But testing is not teaching. If we want to help our learners to improve in accuracy and self-expression we need to go further.

It is in allowing learners to focus on the *process* of writing and the process of learning *through* writing that the computer offers real advantages. Very much as professional writers do, learners can hammer in a first draft of a text, without worrying about errors, and then get feedback on what they have written from their teacher and/or classmates. With the feedback in mind, learners can go back to their screen and process their texts. These further drafts can be done in various stages and in various methodological forms. The possibility of getting the corrections on to paper immediately and being able to make any further changes without having to rewrite the whole text fosters in learners a playful and experimental attitude towards their own texts.

Consequently, in setting up this trial unit we focused on using the computer primarily to facilitate *process-oriented writing*. Unlike the other units in this book, we did not design this unit to be taught over several separate, short lessons, but as an option during four days of a project workshop (with four forty-five minute lessons per day). Such 'project weeks' as they are sometimes called are normally held about once a year in many European schools. They allow teachers and students to focus on an area of teaching and learning without the constraints of their everyday timetables. This permits deeper and more prolonged work in the chosen area. However, the workshop outlined here could also be done as a series of lessons, or you could just try parts of it. Because of this we have decided to present the individual stages of the whole workshop as separable modules. As it happens, most of these are practicable even without a computer – it's just that the redrafting takes longer with pen and paper.

SUMMARY OF MODULES
A Getting to know the computer

1 Mapping the week

2 CALL word game
Introduce and, if necessary, explain relevant CALL words. Quickly delete the words from the board or cover them up. The students key in as many words as they can recall.

3 Component words
Write a word on the board. The students form as many words as they can with its letters.

4 Linking letters
Present a diagram (see Fig. 9.1) and students find as many hidden words as possible.

B Writing activities

5 A picture story
Students find a new ending to a given story. Prompt: an initial (or last) sentence.

6 A guided fantasy and text production
Guide students into and out of a fantasy. The students write a narrative text based on their fantasies.

7 Quadrophonic dictation
The class forms four groups and each group selects a caller. The four callers stand in the four corners of the room. Each group stands in the corner opposite its caller. All the callers dictate to their groups at the same time who key in their text.

8 Jogging dictation
Four copies of the same text are stuck in the opposite corner from each group. Joggers have to run to their text and back to their group, remember as much as they can and dictate the text bit-wise to their group.

C Further writing activities

9 Writing a mini-saga
The students write a text of exactly fifty words.

10 Writing poetry
Give a key word, and students collect associations starting with each letter of the key word or write a free poem.

11 Workshop newspaper
Students compile a newspaper. The newspapers are photocopied and distributed among learners and their colleagues.

Steps towards process orientation

These activities were each done several times during the workshop, whenever the teacher felt they were necessary.

1 Evaluative texts
Students write their feelings about each stage and about the whole workshop.

2 Draft writing
The students write a first draft and print it out. They get feedback from their classmates and/or from the teacher. The focus is on the process of incorporating this feedback into a new draft, not so much on the text as a first-time product.

3 Meta-discussions

When necessary, the teacher gets the students away from the computers for discussion about the progress of their work or the course.

4 Display of texts on a board and/or in a workshop newspaper

Each student can also take home a selection of texts from those displayed.

A GETTING TO KNOW THE COMPUTER

This first phase was absolutely essential in our class since the students were completely unfamiliar with computers. The aim of this introductory phase was twofold: (1) acquisition of basic computer handling skills, and (2) making sure that students had the language needed later to talk about computing matters in English, not their mother tongue.

1 Mapping the week

The teacher asked the twelve students of this group to sit in a circle in the middle of the classroom. There were three computers along each of the longer sides of the room. The teacher gave the students a brief overview of what the next four days would entail. He stressed the fact that they were supposed to speak English as much as possible and added that this required some new words and phrases.

2 CALL word game

The teacher wrote the following words and expressions on the board and tried to elicit their meaning from the learners:

keyboard	*monitor*	*to save*
keys	*file*	*to delete*
word processor	*cursor*	*to insert*
printer	*to load*	*to print out*
floppy disk	*to type in*	
disk drive	*typing error*	

When either a student or the teacher had explained each item, he asked the students to remember as many of them as possible without writing anything down, and then abruptly erased them all.

He put the students in pairs and showed them how to switch on the computers and install their word-processing software. Since none of the students had had any experience with computing or word processing and hardly any of them knew how to type, we had selected very simple software. (This was ZAVATEX, a word-processing package especially designed for use with beginners. It combines the functions of a simple typewriter with the basic advantages of a word processor. It was written by Peter Zavarsky.)

The teacher now handed out a floppy disk to each pair of students. The pairs left the circle of chairs in the middle and, clearly intrigued, began their encounter with the new machine. It was surprising how easy it was for them to take the first step. Within a few minutes all the students had successfully installed the software.

The teacher announced a vocabulary game through which the students would learn the basic functions of the word-processing software.

The students had to type in as many of the words as possible that the teacher had written on the board at the beginning of the lesson.

The winners would be the pair that successfully printed out the largest number of words. There was no time limit because working with a computer for the first time frequently puts users under a certain amount of pressure which we didn't want to add to. Pairs could ask for help from the teacher whenever they wanted.

Stimulated by the competitive nature of the activity, the students started typing away. The teacher walked from pair to pair but without intervening. After a short time students started asking questions such as:

'What can we do? We have just made a typing error. How can we correct it?'

'We want to go into the next line. How can we do that?'

'We had four words on the monitor already. They have all gone.' (This pair had deleted their file.)

'We want to print out our words. Can you help us, please?'

'We have forgotten the *to* in front of *load*. How can we insert it?'

The teacher reminded the students to add their names before or after their texts and, after a quarter of an hour or so, all the students had handed in their print-outs. The teacher checked them quickly and announced the winners.

The teacher then began the instructions for the next activity, but noticed that hardly any of the students were paying any attention. Most were playing around with their keyboards. This gave the teacher a bit of a fright. Maybe the game they'd just done had been too simple and they were bored? Maybe it would have been better to give them a mini-lecture about how to handle the computer and start right away with 'real work'? He ventured the question:

Teacher　*How do you feel about what we have been doing?*
Student 1　*It's fine.*
Student 2　*Yes, it's great fun.*
Student 3　*I thought it would take a lot longer to learn to write with a computer.*

The students seemed totally unaware of the teacher's anxiety. They were hooked on the new medium and their speed in coming to grips with it appeared to have deepened their fascination. The teacher was greatly relieved to learn that they were actually enjoying the work. What he decided for himself, however, was to get the students away from their computers and sitting in the middle of the room whenever he needed their attention. Indeed, this strategy proved very helpful in the following three days. And, unlike shouting or scolding the students for not paying attention, it preserved everyone's good humour.

The following two activities are additional games that aim at improving the students' word-processing skills.

3 Component words

The teacher went to the board and wrote the word *breakfast*. He asked the students to type in as many words as possible using the letters of the word on the board. Again, no time limit was given, but this time the students were not supposed to print out their word lists.

When everyone had finished, the teacher asked one pair after another to read out a word from their list. Pair 1 started with *freak*. The teacher wrote it on the board to allow the students to check spelling. He then asked every pair who had this word in their list to delete it from their screen. This was to familiarise the class with the move for deleting a word from a text. This went on until only one pair still had any words on their screen.

4 Linking letters

To give the students further practice in word-processing skills, the teacher handed out a diagram (Fig. 9.1).

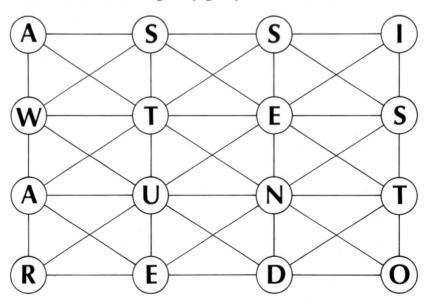

Figure 9.1

The students' task was to make as many words as possible from the letters that link up, for example, *test, aunt, red, send*, etc.

B WRITING ACTIVITIES

5 A picture story

The next activity did not, initially, involve use of the computer. Its purpose was twofold: (1) to get the students away from the screens for a while, and (2) to prepare them for the text production to come.

First the teacher told the class he was going to briefly present the first picture of a picture story on the OHP. He put the picture (Fig. 9.2) on the OHP and switched it on for maybe half a second.

G Gerngross, H Puchta and M Schratz, 'The ice cream man', in *What's the Story*, Spectra 1989. This is a collection of picture stories on mini-transparencies

Figure 9.2

The students were surprised at the brevity of the glimpse, and even more surprised when the teacher asked them what they had seen. A short period of silence followed. Then a few people started guessing:

Student 1 *I think it was snowing.*
Teacher *Snowing? Sorry, it wasn't snowing at all.*
Student 2 *I think I saw a room.*
Teacher *Aha. What sort of room was it?*
Student 2 *No idea.*
Student 3 *I don't know. I think a dining room.*
Teacher *No.*
Student 4 *A bathroom? (Teacher gestures 'No')*
Student 5 *A children's room?*
Student 6 *Maybe a garage.*
Student 7 *A bedroom?*

Teacher   *Right.*
Student 5 *I could see 'ding dong'.*
Teacher   *Aha. What's that? What do you think?*
Student 5 *A bell?*
Teacher   *What sort of bell?*
Student 5 *A church bell.*
Teacher   *No.*
Student 8 *Ah. Somebody came to visit. It was the doorbell and I think a man and a woman were sleeping in bed and they were wake up by the bell.*
Teacher   *You are right. Somebody was sleeping. But it was only a man, and he was woken up by the doorbell. It wasn't a visit though. Look.*

The teacher put the second picture (Fig. 9.3) on the OHP. He had covered it with a sheet of paper in which there was a very small hole. As he moved the sheet slowly over the transparency, details of the picture appeared, disappeared, and reappeared. This triggered off a flurry of guesses.

Student 6 *I think it's the newspaper boy. (Teacher gestures 'No')*
Student 3 *I think I know it. The man has sleeping too long.*
Teacher   *Ah, he has overslept, you mean.*
Student 3 *Yes and so a man from his job, from where he works, has come.*
Student 2 *A colleague.*
Student 3 *Yes, a colleague has come and wants to wake him up.*
etc.

Finally the teacher removed the sheet of paper and showed the whole picture, together with the first one, to the class:

Figure 9.3   *ibid.*

Teacher   *I'd like you to close your eyes now. Imagine that you can see the next two pictures of the story. I'll give you two or three minutes . . .*

The students closed their eyes. Some of them had already begun to rest on their arms, others sat with their backs straight. All remained silent. After two or three minutes the teacher started again.

Teacher   *Well, perhaps you know how the story continues. Don't tell us anything about what you imagined. Instead, I'd like you to ask me questions about the next two pictures to find out what's in them. OK? (Students nod their heads)*

Teacher   *What about Picture 3? What happened? I'll only answer with 'Yes' or 'No'.*

Student 9   *Has the man spoken to the ice cream man?*

Teacher   *(goes to the board and notes down) Did the man . . .?*

Student 9   *Oh yes, sorry. Did he speak to him?*

Teacher   *Yes.*

Student 9   *Did he tell him to go away?*

Teacher   *No.*

Student 10   *Did the man shout at him?*

Teacher   *No.*

Student 4   *Has the man buy some ice cream? (Teacher points to the prompt* Did the man . . .?*)*
Ah. Did the man . . . uhh . . . bought . . .

Teacher   *. . . buy . . .*

Student 4   *. . . buy some ice cream?*

Teacher   *Yes.*

etc.

The same procedure was applied with the next picture and finally the teacher presented Pictures 3 and 4 to the class (Figs. 9.4 and 9.5).

ibid.   Figure 9.4

Figure 9.5

ibid.

The teacher then switched off the OHP and asked the students to get together in pairs and think of a possible ending to the story. The teacher asked several pairs about their endings. Then he presented Pictures 5 and 6 (Figs. 9.6 and 9.7) on the OHP, to general amusement.

Figure 9.6

ibid.

ibid.   Figure 9.7

The teacher then asked the students to concentrate on the whole set of pictures for a short time and, while the OHP was still on, asked them to sit in groups. He gave each group a set of slips of paper which he had prepared before the lesson (Fig. 9.8).

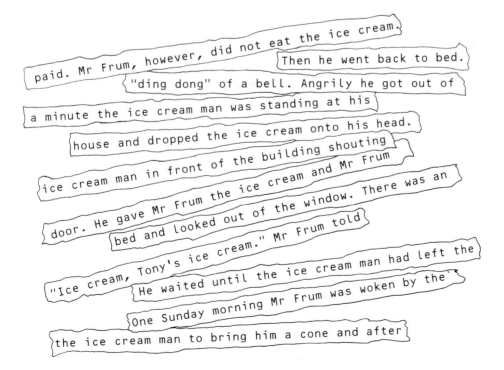

Figure 9.8

Without asking the students to read the story out, the teacher collected the slips of paper. The teacher then presented the following skeleton text on a large sheet of paper stuck up on the board:

```
O . . S . . . . . m . . . . . . M. F . . . w . w . . . b . t . .'d . . . d . . .'o . a
b . . . .A . . . . . . h . g . . o . . o . b . . a . . l . . . . o . . o . t . . w . . . . . .
T . . . . w . . a . i . . c . . . . m . . s . . . . . . . .,'l . . c . . . !' M . F . . . t . . .
t . . m . . t . b . . . . h . . a c . . . . T . . m . . g . . . M. F . . . t . . i . . c . . . .
a . . M. F . . . p . . . . M. F . . . d . . n . . e . . t . . i . c . . . . . W . . .
t . . i . . c . . . . m . . h . . l . . . t . . h . . . . ,h . d . . . . . i . o . h . . h . . . .
T . . . h . w . . . b . . . t . b . . .
```

It was fascinating to watch the students begin reconstructing the text in groups of two or three with no instruction from the teacher.

A similar activity ('Storyboard') can be found in Morgan and Rinvolucri's *Vocabulary* (1986). It could of course be done on a word processor with a text reconstruction program.

After the students had reconstructed the text, the teacher asked them to go back to their word processors and write a story beginning with the sentence: 'Next Sunday Mr Frum was woken by the ice cream man's bell again . . .'

In pairs again, the students started writing their texts. Whenever a pair finished, the teacher got them to print out their first draft and he checked it for errors. To encourage habits of redrafting and self-correction, he underlined problematic areas in pencil, adding margin notes or abbreviations such as V for vocabulary, SP for spelling, G for grammar. The students then went through their texts again, trying to correct them on the screen. By the second draft most students had successfully corrected about two-thirds of their errors. The teacher pointed out the remaining errors in the same way. When their texts were ready (after three drafts, in most cases), the students fixed them to a display board and then strolled round reading each other's texts. Figure 9.9 shows one of their stories:

Figure 9.9

```
Next Sunday Mr Frum was woken by the ice cream man's bell again. He
got up and looked out of the window. He got very angry. Then he
quietly went into the kitchen. There he took a bowl of honey. He
went back to his bedroom and opened the window. Without looking
down he spilled the honey out of the window. He didn't see that
the ice cream man was not there any more. There was now the postman
standing. The postman shouted, "What's this? Ughh, honey! Wait a
moment and I'll call the police. They'll take you to prison." Five
minutes later the police arrived. The policeman looked up to Mr
Frum's window, down at the postman and suddenly he began to
laugh ...
```

Here the first day ended. There was general voicing of surprise (from the teacher, ourselves and the students themselves) at how quickly they had got used to the computer work. The attention paid by the teacher to clarity of instruction and the variation of activity seemed to have played a role in this. Particularly helpful in maintaining focus and pace seemed to be the practice of getting learners into a new seating arrangement well away from their computers during phases when instructions were being given.

It was also surprising to see how many of the errors in their stories they were able to correct themselves in the second draft. In fact, very few errors remained to be corrected by the teacher after the third draft.

6 A guided fantasy and text production

At the beginning of the second day the teacher started with an evaluation of the first day. He asked the students to write a short account of the first day's activities, including their own feelings about them if they wanted to. Again, these texts were put on the display board. After everyone had read their colleagues' texts, the class sat in a discussion circle.

Teacher   *Well, you have read the other texts now. What's your reaction?*

Student 1   *Fine. I think it is very good what we do here.*

Teacher   *What is it you like about it?*

Student 1   *I think it is good that we have more time for what we do than normally. It is good because we can really also speak about our texts for example.*

Student 2   *I like the writing together. It's good because you . . . if I have not a good idea U helps me and then I think of something again and so on.*

Teacher   *What I like a lot is the fact that you seem to try to talk English all the time.*

Student 3   *Yes, but it's difficult . . . uhh . . . yesterday I write a text and then it was away . . .*

Teacher   *You mean you lost it? Did you delete it?*

Student 3   *Yes, I mean I don't know. We didn't delete it. It was just . . . uhh . . .*

Teacher   *Gone?*

Student 3   *Yes.*

Teacher   *And so what did you do?*

Student 4   *We have write it again and then we have lost it again.*

Teacher   *Oh no!*

Student 4   *Yes, and then we spoke a lot of German.*

The teacher used this discussion phase as a lead-in to the next writing activity: writing a text in connection with a fantasy trip.

Teacher   *I'd like to read out to you now a text that a student in one of my classes wrote a few years ago. This student was also fourteen, like most of you. I'd like you to listen to this text and then I'd like you to guess what kind of situation the writer of this text was in before he or she wrote this text.*

(starts reading) It was a quiet day. I was walking and dancing through a meadow. The sun was shining and many birds were flying through the air. Sometimes leaves from trees were dancing around me. But I was not happy. I was sad and thinking about a problem. I looked down on the ground. There was a little river.

I stood there for a while and thought about the problem. Then I went on, and after some time I started running through a wet meadow. Suddenly, I saw a rainbow. The sun was shining warmly and when I could feel the warmth of the sun on my skin, I began to feel happy again. I did not think of my problem any more.

The teacher silently waited for the class to react. One of the girls started things off:

Student 1   *Was this a girl or a boy which wrote this text?*

Teacher   *What do you think? Can you guess? I mean what do you think? What kind of person was this?*

Student 2   *I think it was a girl. And I think a boy is not so romantic. I think she has a very good – uhh – what's Vorstellungskraft in English?*

Teacher   *Imagination.*

Student 3   *Why do you think it is a girl? I think a boy can also have this.*

Student 2   *I don't know. I think girls are more romantic. (laughs)*

Teacher   *(to S3) Do you sometimes have such fantasies? Daydreams?*

Student 3   *Yes, very often.*

Teacher   *When?*

Student 3   *(laughs) In the maths lesson.*

Teacher   *And in the English lessons?*

Student 4   *Yes. (laughs) When it's boring. Then I think of holidays and I forget all.*

Teacher   *That's very practical. You just have a daydream and you forget the world around you? Is that the same with everybody?*

Students   *Yes . . . sometimes . . . (several students at the same time)*

Student 5   *I never make a daydream . . . I am very . . . realistisch.*

Teacher   *Down-to-earth.*

Student 5   *Yes.*

Teacher   *I see. Well, what I did with the class the girl was in who wrote this text was that I played some music to them and I told them something, kind of a story, you know . . . if you want to we can do the same thing. Would you like that?*

Students   *Yes.*

Teacher   *(has switched on the cassette recorder, soft music gently wafts into the room) With your eyes open or closed . . . allow yourself just to focus on your sitting position . . . and while you are doing this . . . becoming aware of any changes you'd like to make . . . in order to . . . relax and go a bit deeper . . . maybe you can . . . while you are listening . . . to this tape . . . just focus on the rhythm of your breath . . . without making it faster or slower . . . just listen as it comes and goes . . . and while you are doing this . . . maybe you can imagine . . . while you are listening to the sound of this music . . . just to relax . . . that whenever you breathe out . . . you are getting rid of all the stress that you might feel . . . whereas whenever you breathe in . . . you can imagine that you are taking up fresh new energy . . . now . . . that helps you to . . . relax and enjoy . . . right now . . .*

And while you are doing this . . . in your own time and at your own pace . . . you might want to join in on a short fantasy . . . to a place . . . where you can really relax . . . right now . . . and this place . . . helps you to become calm and relaxed . . . as you go there . . . and it's a very special place . . . just for you . . . and while on the one hand you are listening to this music . . . on the other maybe you can imagine now . . . what this place is going to be like . . . and only you know . . . if you can see any colours in your place . . . if the colours are bright or dark . . . and nobody else knows . . . what else there is in this special place . . . if this place is in the open air . . . or maybe in a room and only you know . . . while you can possibly see things very clearly . . . or rather vaguely . . . what you can hear there . . . in this special place . . . where you can relax . . . maybe it's the sound of the wind . . . or some kind of music . . . soft and warm . . . filling your place now . . . or maybe a human voice . . . singing or talking to you . . . and while you can possibly see and hear things there . . . you can now become aware of your feelings . . . of joy and relaxation . . . and you know . . . that wherever you are . . . this place is there just for you . . . and you are totally safe there . . . now . . . and nobody else knows . . . what you'd like to take with you from this place . . . on a day like today . . . maybe a thing . . . or a sound . . . or just a feeling . . . to remind you of the special experiences you have had . . . while you are now . . . very slowly . . . at your own pace . . . beginning slowly to come back to your classroom . . . and open your eyes again . . . and maybe stretch a little . . . with a special feeling of freshness and joy . . . and while you are listening to the numbers going downwards . . . from ten to one now . . . you'll know that this fantasy has finished when you hear the number one . . . ten . . . nine . . . eight . . . seven . . . six . . . five . . . four . . . three . . . two . . . one.

As time went on, the students seemed to have relaxed more and more. Once, a boy started to giggle and seemed to disturb the girl sitting next to him. When the teacher noticed, he stood up for a minute and put his hand on the boy's shoulder. The boy looked up towards the teacher, obviously feeling guilty and at the same time finding it difficult to repress his need to laugh. The teacher just smiled at him supportively and this evidently allowed the boy to relax again.

Reactions like this are quite normal during a class's first experience with a fantasy journey. We have found in numerous classes, however, that if guided fantasies are done in a caring and respectful way, they can help to improve trust in a class. Furthermore, they can be of great help in developing creativity, language competence and self-esteem.

After the guided fantasy the teacher suggested that the students write a text about their experience. One student at a time worked at the screen while the other sat and watched. The teacher also suggested (1) that each writer should consult their partner in case of any language problems, and (2) that after the writer had printed out the first draft they should give it to their partner for correction and consult the teacher only after the second draft had been printed.

Figure 9.10 is an example of a text created by a student.

Figure 9.10

```
The Wind

I fly high up through the sky
The fresh wind blowing into my face
Suddenly I hear the water splashing
I look up at the big mountains around me
The river is full of life and power
An eagle catches a fat fish and flies up
to the sky
The sun shines and the mountains get a
beautiful red colour
I sit on a big stone, my feet in the
cold water and
the wind is blowing.
```

After finishing writing, the students stuck their texts up on the wall and everybody was asked to read at least five other texts. Then followed a whole class discussion in a big circle. Because each learner had read only *some* of the texts, when one learner commented on a text, other students (who had not read this text) asked questions about it. Thus, based on the principle of information gaps, the discussion was quite animated.

After this discussion the students wrote another evaluative text about what they liked and didn't like about the second day. Figure 9.11 is an excerpt from one student's account of the guided fantasy.

Figure 9.11

```
It was really very, very nice. I enjoyed it very much.
```

7 Quadrophonic dictation

The third day began with a surprise for the teacher. Sitting in a circle with the class again, he wanted to say what he had planned for the day. But things turned out differently:

Teacher   OK, I'd just like to tell you what we are going to do today.
Student 1   Are we writing again a text? (facial expression suggesting that Student 1 is fed up)
Teacher   What do you mean? Don't you like the texts you have written?

Student 1	*Oh yes. Not this. I mean I really like this project. But not writing all the time.*
Teacher	*So?*
Student 2	*I also think so. I think we should play a game again. That was very good on Monday.*
Teacher	*You mean the vocabulary games we played? But I wanted to do these games with you just to help you to learn to write on the computer very quickly.*
Students	*Yes. Can we play this game again?*
Teacher	*You'd like the same game again? Wouldn't this be boring?*
Student 3	*No, that would be good. Or another game. Doesn't matter. Then we can write a text again. But not write texts all the time. This is very . . . what's* anstrengend *in English?*
Teacher	*Tiring.*
Student 3	*Yes, and so we want tiring things and also funny things.*

After the class had played the game 'Component words' from Stage 3 again (this time it was *grandfather* instead of *breakfast*), the teacher introduced some new games that the students seemed to enjoy enormously. First came two different types of dictation.

When the students heard that they were going to write a dictation, they thought the teacher was teasing because they had asked for something *fun*. Only after the teacher promised that the two dictations would indeed be fun and totally different from the 'normal' dictations they did in their German class, did they acquiesce. This is what followed.

The teacher divided the class into four groups of three. Each group sat in front of one of the word processors placed in each of the four corners of the room. The teacher asked each group to send him one member as their 'caller' and explained that the caller should be someone who was quite skilled at reading out loud. Then he asked each of the four callers to stand in the corner of the room opposite the other members of their group – the 'writers'.

The teacher then handed out four different texts of about the same length and roughly the same level of language – one text to each caller. Each caller now had to give this dictation to his or her own group. The teacher told the groups that they would get points both for speed and for good spelling.

Each of the four callers, at the same time, then started to dictate their text to their own group. Although this might sound like a recipe for total chaos, the initial confusion subsided after just a few seconds. By then, each set of writers was able to tune in to their own caller and so filter out most of the interference.

The rules of this activity are:

- The group that finishes first gets four points from the teacher, the one who finishes second three and so on.
- Each group gets time to correct their text, which they then hand in to

the teacher. The teacher checks the spelling, awarding a maximum of ten points for a flawless dictation and subtracting one point for each spelling mistake.

- The points for speed and spelling are then added and indicate the winner.

Comment: Competitions frequently have a negative influence on the social atmosphere of a class. We have found, however, that this form of competition avoids unproductive rivalry which could easily arise within the groups if the focus was on speed only. Since each group has time to go through their text together, the odd weak speller in the group cannot become a scapegoat, since it is up to everybody to contribute to a flawless text.

This form of a dictation has three main objectives:

- The element of having to filter out one listening source from background noise stretches students' abilities to listen attentively to fellow students *in* English.
- It increases the students' awareness of the need for cooperation in group work.
- It helps practise spelling in a natural way.

It also has great potential for fun.

8 Jogging dictation

The students liked the activity above so much that the teacher decided to try another dictation. This time he aimed at increasing the students' concentration, their ability to remember and, again, their awareness of the need to cooperate with each other.

The activity involved each group selecting a 'jogger'. The teacher put up four identical texts, one in each corner of the room, with each group having their text in the opposite corner.

The rules of this activity are:

- At the starting signal the joggers each race to their text. They cannot remove it, but have to try to remember as much of it as they can, word for word.
- They run back to their group, dictate what they can remember and then go back to their text again and try to remember some more.
- Points are given for spelling and speed of completion.

It helps to write on the board or stick up on posters the names of English pronunciation, marks, so the joggers can describe punctuation without falling back into the mother tongue. This is important, because the wish to finish first could easily lead to the students using the language they feel most at ease with. For the same reason it also helps to display or write on the board essential language such as: *Sorry, I didn't get the word after '. . .'; Can you repeat this, please?* etc. (See Davis and Rinvolucri 1988 for other dictation activities.)

C FURTHER WRITING ACTIVITIES

The fact that the teacher readily gave in to the students' suggestion for games cheered them up immensely. The games themselves brought the energy level back up, so that the students were ready for further writing activities.

9 Writing a mini-saga

The first of these writing activities was writing a mini-saga. This a literary form that had its beginnings in a competition run by the *Sunday Telegraph Magazine*. These are the rules:

- Each mini-saga must have exactly fifty words, no more, no less.
- The title cannot have more than five additional words.
- The mini-saga can only be a story – not a poem, joke, or anything else.

Here is an example:

In the Name of Progress

The beautiful village was dying. 'There is no industry,' complained its inhabitants, 'our young people are leaving.' The developers moved in; factories belched out gas and motorways ate into the hedgerows. 'They have destroyed the beauty. We must escape to the unspoiled countryside,' cried the new community – and moved away.

MAUREEN ROBERTS
BOURNEMOUTH

B Aldiss (ed), *The Book of Mini Sagas*, Guemsey Press 1985 p. 174

The production of mini-sagas is ideal for introducing students to process writing since it combines tightness and clarity of structure with wide scope for creativity.

In particular, because they are short and spare, it is easy for students to attain an overview of their structure. And the correction and rewriting involved tends to be quite manageable, even in the beginning.

First the teacher presented a photocopy of a mini-saga as an example and then explained the form. Then, as a further prelude to writing the teacher suggested several general topics (e.g. 'vampires', 'love', 'horror', 'farewell'). (In some cases it helps to present, in addition, a group of words in a scatter pattern for each topic.) The students then worked in pairs to produce the first draft of their mini-saga, which they then revised with input from the teacher. Final versions of all the mini-sagas were then displayed in the classroom.

Here is one fourteen-year-old's mini-saga on the topic 'vampires'.

One day an old and ugly vampire went back to the city. First he went to the graveyard because he wanted to visit his old friends. When they saw him they said: 'Our old friend! Let's have a party! Let's go to the hospital and drink some bottles of blood!'

C Holzmann,' Washu fruit and vampires – Mini-sagas im Englischunterricht', in *Unser Weg*, 1, 1989 pp. 19–21

10 Writing poetry

Day 4 started with another activity the students seemed to like a lot. First the teacher asked them to come to the board and write words which they associated with a given word or phrase, in this case *learning English*. Then the teacher asked them first to write the word vertically down the left of their screen and then write, horizontally, a word or words on each line starting with the first letter given. Again, the learners enjoyed the opportunity to play around with language in a way which made it possible for them to delete and replace words much more often and easily than with pen and paper.

A popular variation was writing down their thoughts and feelings about a given topic (e.g. 'computers') in poetic form. Figures 9.12 and 9.13 are examples of each idea.

```
Lesson
Englishbook
Angry children
Reading a summary
New English teacher
Grammar
End of the English lesson
No good mark
Great lesson
Learn for the test
Irregular verbs
Silly children
Homework

            (Ulrike)
```

Figure 9.12

```
Computer

When I hear the word computer I think of many words
                              I also think of playing games
                              often it is very interesting
                              but sometimes it is boring
                              I think of work in a big room,
                              many people are working there
                              I also think of a hectic atmosphere


If I got a computer           I would be very happy about it

                              I could play and write with it
                              My friends could also play funny
                              games on the computer
    If                                               it.
       I                                      on
         really                            things
             got                     these
               a              all
                 computer        do
                   I would
```

Figure 9.13

11 Workshop newspaper

When the teacher suggested that the students put together a newspaper containing some of the texts produced during the workshop they reacted enthusiastically. In order to save time, this was done in a rather old-fashioned way, with no attempt at 'desk top publishing', which would have demanded software and software skills far above the competence of the learners in the trial class.

First, students decided on the texts they wanted to be 'published', cut them out and pasted them on A4 sheets. These were then photo-copied, together with a cover created by one student with artistic flair. Finally, copies of the newspaper were distributed to the students who had taken part in projects other then the text-writing workshop. This proved very valuable. On the one hand, the workshop paper amounted to a self-assessment for the participants on their work, and on the other hand they had something to show their classmates involved in other projects.

CONCLUDING DISCUSSION

Following our workshop, the trial class began to use the computer as a writing tool in their regular English classes. There were some problems, though, as the teacher commented:

Several times, when I wanted to use the computer lab, there was a colleague who wanted it for her class too. The fact that we have to leave our regular classroom and move to the computer lab just for a fifty-minute lesson means that we lose

quite a lot of time. The resulting time pressure does not facilitate an atmosphere of creativity. Sometimes we'd just like to use a word processor for a very short period of time, but there's no point in moving the whole class to the computer lab for that, so I just get the learners to do the writing by hand.

This is a typical practical obstacle to the integration of computer work into language learning. Obviously, it is a matter of finance as to whether there can be computers (maybe lap-tops) readily available for use in every classroom. But without such ready and flexible availability, the temptation exists – when one does have the use of a computer room – to use the computers so intensively that they control language learning and, ultimately, threaten to drain it of interest. Our advice is to break up computer work with plenty of non-CALL activity.